ORGANIC
MARIN

ORGANIC
MARIN

RECIPES FROM LAND TO TABLE

BY TIM PORTER & FARINA WONG KINGSLEY

PRODUCED BY MARIN MAGAZINE

PHOTOGRAPHS BY TIM PORTER

**Andrews McMeel
Publishing, LLC**
Kansas City

Organic Marin: Recipes from Land to Table

Copyright © 2008 by Marin Magazine

Photographs copyright © 2008 by Tim Porter

Design: Jennifer Barry Design, Fairfax, California
Production Assistance: Kristen Hall
Food Styling: Jackie Slade

08 09 10 11 12 TWP 10 9 8 7 6 5 4 3 2 1

Library of Congress Cataloging-in-Publication Data

Porter, Tim.
  Organic Marin : recipes from land to table / by Tim Porter and Farina Wong Kingsley ; produced by Marin Magazine ; photographs by Tim Porter. — 1st ed.
    p. cm.
  Includes index.
  ISBN-13: 978-0-7407-7314-3
  ISBN-10: 0-7407-7314-3
  1. Cookery, American–California style. 2. Cookery–California–Marin County. 3. Natural foods. I. Kingsley, Farina Wong. II. Marin Magazine. II. Title.

TX715.2.C34P67   2008
641.59794'62–dc22

                    2008003435

www.andrewsmcmeel.com

Attention: Schools and Businesses
Andrews McMeel books are available at quantity discounts with bulk purchase for educational, business, or sales promotional use. For information, please write to:
Special Sales Department, Andrews McMeel Publishing, LLC, 1130 Walnut Street

contents

spring

summer

fall

winter

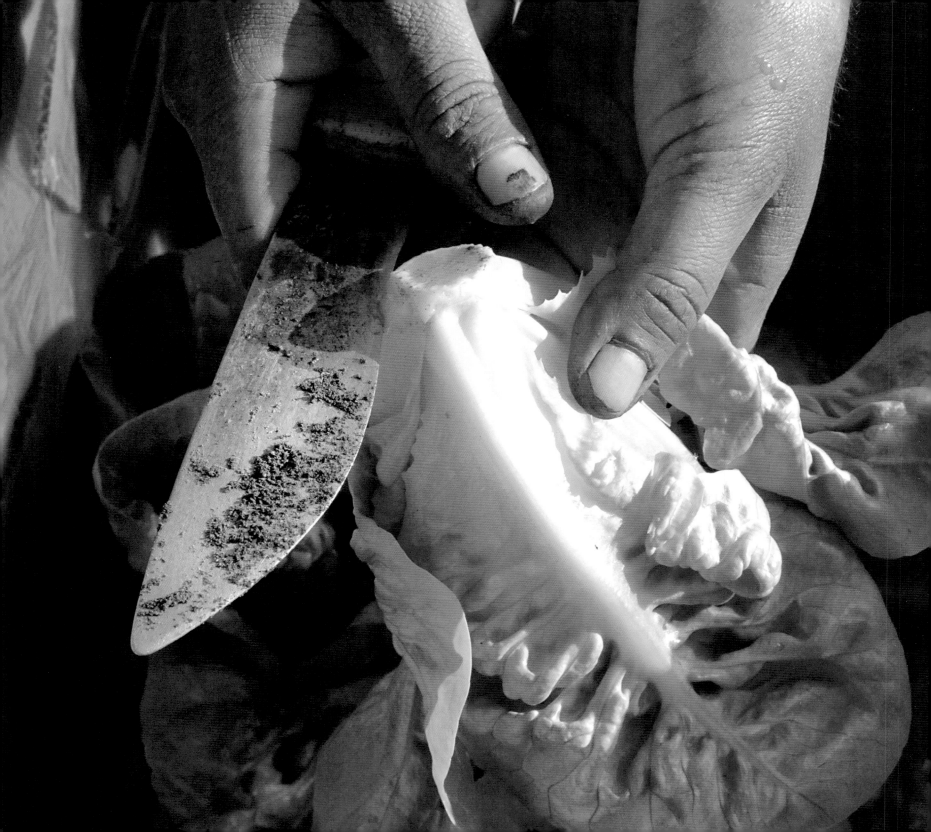

Food is our common ground, a universal experience.
—James Beard

Organic Marin *by Tim Porter*

Janet Brown of Allstar Organics leads a tour of her farm in Lagunitas sponsored by Marin Organic.

Food fosters community. That's what Mickey Murch says. He's a young organic farmer from Bolinas, the tiny Marin County town that, as much as any place in California, embraced the practices of organic farming long before it was fashionable. They're just three little words. But they encompass a huge idea: the connection between food and community, between farmer and family, between land and table. The passionate belief in that link—a link missing in much of today's commodity-based agribusiness—nourishes Marin's organic movement, making it not only a source of fresh, healthy food for the San Francisco Bay Area, but also a wellspring of innovative, sustainable farming practices that have been copied throughout the world.

This book was inspired by that idea and the many people who make it a daily reality here in Marin County. Those of us who live here know that we are fortunate. Year-round we can shop in farmers' markets and buy just-harvested food directly from the person who pulled it from the ground. Our region's local restaurants—from the internationally famous, like Chez Panisse in Berkeley and Slanted Door in San Francisco, to the ultra local, like Rustic Bakery in Larkspur and Small Shed Flatbreads in Mill Valley—have menus that feature organic produce and dairy products that have traveled only hours, not days or weeks, to their kitchens. Beef and hog ranchers produce flavor-filled cuts of meat from animals that have been naturally raised and have lived a full, organic life.

We are fortunate, indeed, to live amid such plenty, to be able to taste the best the Earth has to offer, and to enjoy the fruits of the hard work of farm labor done by people who believe that feeding good food to their community will make the world a better place. This book, *Organic Marin: Recipes from Land to Table,* celebrates that effort and that hope.

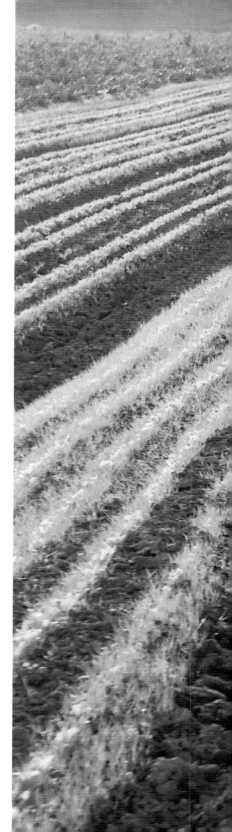

Organic farming pioneers Dennis Dierks *(left)* of Paradise Valley Produce and Warren Weber of Star Route Farms, both in Bolinas.

In the Beginning

Marin's organic roots reach back more than thirty years to the days when young idealists like Warren Weber and Dennis Dierks put their postsixties values about clean living, community, and collective effort into action in West Marin. They bought land and started farming organically, learning one crop at a time how to work with nature rather than against it.

Today, Weber and Dierks are still growing organic food, and many others have joined them. Their farms, Star Route Farms and Paradise Valley Produce, are two of more than sixty certified organic food producers in Marin. Their products range from row crops of nearly every type of vegetable to cool-weather fruit; farmhouse cheeses, yogurt, and other dairy goods; and pasture-raised pork and beef.

Even that extensive list, though, doesn't fully describe the variety produced by Marin's organic farmers. Allstar Organics in Nicasio and Lagunitas, for example, grows more than two dozen types of tomatoes. Little Organic Farm in Tomales plants more than twenty types of potatoes, and Paradise Valley Produce in Bolinas has more than a dozen varieties of lettuce in the field. Fresh Run Farm in Bolinas has heirloom apple trees dating back more than half a century. Not only are the organic buyers of Marin eating chemical-free food, they're treating their taste buds to flavors that can only come from specialty growers whose livelihood depends not on mass production but on quality and uniqueness.

In some ways, Marin County was an unlikely candidate to become the nation's organic-farming standard bearer. The smallest in size and population of the counties that contain the 7 1/2 million people in the Bay Area, it is usually seen as a place of quaint tourist attractions like the bayside town of Sausalito, or natural wonders like the towering redwood groves of Muir Woods. Just minutes from San Francisco over the Golden Gate Bridge, Marin attracts hikers and mountain bikers to the trails of 2,571-foot Mt. Tamalpais, strollers and beachcombers to its wild western beaches, and backpackers and day-trippers to the magnificent parklands of the Point Reyes National Seashore.

Even though more than 50 percent of Marin is designated open space, to the casual observer the most visible signs of agriculture are the pastoral scenes of cows wandering the hillsides of West Marin. Indeed, 99 percent of the agricultural land in Marin is pasture that feeds more than thirty thousand head of cattle, sheep, and goats. Row crops—the lettuce, chard, beets, cabbage, and carrots that entice buyers at local farmers' markets—represent only 1 percent of the county's farmland.

It is a wonder, then, that from this small slice of land such a big idea sprung. "It didn't happen by chance," says Warren Weber. "It happened because people were doing creative things."

Not just people. Marin benefits from a perfect storm of collaboration between farmers, local government and consumers. "First and foremost," says Helge Hellberg, executive director of Marin Organic, an advocacy and education organization of local and organic farmers and ranchers, "we have some of the best agricultural producers in Marin County, people who are true environmental stewards."

Scenes from land to market: A picturesque dairy farm nestled in a valley east of Novato *(left)*; *(above)* farmer Jesse Kuhn of Marin Roots Farms works his ten-acre field; and a local produce farmer cuts sweet organic peaches for customers to taste at the Marin County Farmers' Market.

Farmers' markets are a ritual in every Marin community. Star Route Farms in Bolinas even puts out an unattended roadside farm stand, where buyers pay on the honor system.

Also, says Hellberg, "besides the high level of eco-literate people in Marin County, Marin is the closest bread basket to San Francisco, a food-oriented city with chefs who understand the difference between really good food and really good organic food, and with people who are willing to pay a little bit more and get a superb product that is healthier and protects the environment as well as our local communities at the same time."

Finally, he says, Marin has Stacy Carlsen, one of the most progressive agricultural commissioners in the nation, someone dedicated to providing farmers with the knowledge and the governmental infrastructure necessary to succeed.

A Community of Values

In this age of large food companies and supersized retailers embracing organic food production and sales, there is little doubt that the underlying values of environmental sustainability and community connection that drew Warren Weber and Dennis Dierks back to the land in the 1970s continue to flourish in Marin. A conversation with Stacy Carlsen affirms the idea. To him, organic food is the critical ingredient in the three-legged platform that supports a sustainable community.

"The key factor is that organic food products, as a general rule, are sold locally," says Carlsen. "That is really the critical aspect we're trying to develop. The local food, local consumption, model is critical to long-term economic sustainability on the farm."

Local organic food, and what farmers and ranchers call "value-added products" such as cheese, jams, and salad mixes sold directly to the consumer, can command higher prices in the market. This means that small-scale family farmers can break out of the cycle of earning less and less each year for their work as large-scale commodity agribusinesses push down prices.

Quite simply, no matter how committed a farmer might be to long-term environmental values, he or she needs sufficient income to keep the farm going. As Dennis Dierks of Paradise Valley Produce puts it, "You can't be sustainable if you can't stay in business." A successful family farm, selling locally, allows farmers the opportunity to develop the other elements of a holistic sustainable community: cultural sustainability, or the preservation of family on the farm; social sustainability, or being able to pay workers a just wage; and environmental sustainability, or the protection and enrichment of the land.

"The West Marin farmers know there is a community of values that support the farm and the farm process," says Carlsen. And, both figuratively and literally, beneath those values is respect for the land, the soil. This is the thing organic advocates speak about most fervently.

"Every society is a direct reflection of the status of its soil," says Hellberg of Marin Organic, "so any poisoned soil, any sterile soil, like we have so much of in the United States, will be reflected in the community. Everything comes from soil, food for us, feed for the animals, and fiber for clothing. We are nothing without soil. In Marin County, we saw the warning signs early enough to reverse that trend and build a community on healthy soil. We are building soil, we are building relationships, we are building infrastructure, and developing new markets. We are changing the existing paradigm."

Marin Organic sponsors a seasonal farmers' market at Toby's Feed Barn in Point Reyes Station where customers can purchase a variety of organic food products all from Marin.

Strawberries in the field *(above)* at Sartori Farm near Tomales, and later at a farmers' market. In nearby Nicasio, one-room St. Mary's Church *(right)* has been a local Marin landmark since 1867.

Thirty years ago, the future looked ominous for agriculture in Marin. Local dairies were closing, small farmers were going out of business, and land developers were hungrily eying the farmland of West Marin as potential sites for entire new cities.

At one point, plans were even afoot to build a city of 125,000 people on the shores of Tomales Bay in the heart of Marin's dairy country. Local farmers and ranchers fought back, and one of their primary weapons was MALT, the Marin Agricultural Land Trust.

Cofounded by Ellen Straus, the late matriarch of the family that now operates the organic Straus Family Creamery, MALT buys development rights from local landowners, preserving the land for agricultural uses. Since its founding in 1980, MALT has protected thirty-eight thousand acres of land.

The lesson, as MALT points out in a quote from biologist Phyllis Faber, another cofounder of the organization, is that "you can have a vision of what you want the future to look like, and you can make it happen."

A Future of Promise and Hope

The public's appetite for healthy—and tasty—naturally produced food is growing. Larger environmental concerns, some on a planetary level, are causing individuals and families to ask: What can we do? One answer is buy organic, locally grown food from farmers who believe their responsibility is to enhance the soil, not deplete it; to work in partnership with nature, not overcome it; and to make use of all elements in the farming process, not discard them as waste.

❦ Marin Agricultural ❧
Land Trust

Best known by its acronym MALT, the Marin Agricultural Land Trust was born in 1980 as local ranchers and conservationists fought plans for massive suburban development of West Marin farmlands. MALT negotiates with landowners to create conservation easements that keep lands in permanent agricultural use. Today, MALT's easements, many of them identified by roadside signs, total nearly 40,000 acres. The organization also offers a variety of educational programs, including farm tours, lectures, and hikes.

✎ Marin Organic ✎

An organization of more than forty farmers and ranchers, Marin Organic is the most visible voice of the Marin organic food community. Formed in 1999 as an advocacy group for organic farming, Marin Organic now offers tours of farms and ranches and consumer education programs, sponsors an organic school lunch initiative that feeds over 12,000 children a week in local schools, and runs a weekly summer farmers' market in Point Reyes Station in which all the vendors come from within twenty miles of the market. (More information at *www.marinorganic.com*.)

Cow manure can power a farm (as it does at Straus Family Creamery). A solar array can cut dependency on the utility grid (as it does at Star Route Farm). A horse ranch can provide fertilizer for a tomato farm (as it does for Allstar Organics). And blemished produce, good enough to eat but difficult to sell, can provide healthy lunches for twelve thousand schoolchildren a week (as it does in Marin County, under a program started by Marin Organic in partnership with local public schools and farmers).

"Let us come to work with a sense of amazing abundance," says Hellberg of Marin Organic. "If there's anything you have, we'll make use of it. Nature has provided more than we can ever use or ever need. The solutions to most if not all of our challenges are already out there if we can get away from consumption and waste and change our mind set."

One of Marin Organic's goals is to make Marin an organic county. That day may be a long way off, if indeed it ever comes. In the meantime, though, says Weber of Star Route, "we're trying to produce as sustainable a county as possible.

"Through this networking of public and private organizations, of producers and consumers, we have created a model for other areas. We have been able, all of us together, to create a system and environment for sustainable agriculture to have a successful role in the community."

A cow leaves the milking station at Straus Family Creamery; dumping horse manure in a field at an Allstar Organics field in Nicasio; using solar panels to power operations at Star Route Farms in Bolinas (above).

About half the land in Marin County is agricultural. Efforts by the Marin Agricultural Land Trust (MALT) and other advocates to keep this farmland open mean that only minutes north of the congested streets of San Francisco it's possible to find scenes like this one—Hicks Valley Road stretching colorfully into the sunset.

Marin's organic community rose to front-page fame in 2005, when Prince Charles of England and his wife, Camilla, the Duchess of Cornwall, visited Point Reyes Station and Bolinas with Hellberg as their guide, chatting their way through a local farmers' market and having lunch with Weber and other local farmers.

That type of attention helps spread Marin's message, says Hellberg. "We have the opportunity to change the world forever," he says. "We have international guests who look at Marin as a model. They're coming for the agriculture, but what they're attracted to is the hope we've created here. This is a county of hope."

There's one more thing. Amid discussions about the economics of organic farming, the quality of fresh food, and the good intentions of lofty social goals, it's important not to lose track of one basic component in Marin's organic story: a group of people who like to grow things and, despite the endless work, the annual financial uncertainty, and the vagaries of crop-wilting weather, lettuce-munching deer, and chicken-chomping coyotes, who have a good time doing it—perhaps now more than ever.

"I feel like when I was a kid back in the seventies," says Weber, "because in Marin County we now have all this wonderful excitement. We now have people growing things they have never grown before. We're in a cycle that is really wonderful. We're having a lot of fun."

Janet Brown *(left)* in her expansive herb garden at Allstar Organics. Her partner, Marty Jacobsen *(right)*, packs heirloom tomatoes at his field in Nicasio.

Allstar Organics

Marin's Organic Farms

Allstar Organics began in 1994 when Marty Jacobsen and Janet Brown planted what they called a "vineyard" of heirloom tomatoes in a sunny one-acre field next to their home in Lagunitas, a small town on the edge of Marin's redwood forest.

Today, that terraced field is filled with organic lavender, rosemary, spearmint, Thai basil, cilantro, and other herbs that Janet dries and sells alone or mixed with salt. Sharing the field are five hundred antique rose bushes, whose colorful petals Janet distills to make a delicately flavored rose sugar and refreshing hydrosols.

A few years ago, Marty began working a ten-acre piece of land in Nicasio, just over the hill from Lagunitas. There, he continues to grow tomatoes—twenty varieties of heirlooms, cherries, and others—and has had room to expand to other organic produce, including winter squash, watermelon, strawberries, cantaloupe, tomatillos, zucchini, eggplant, and five kinds of beans. Marty is known among Bay Area chefs as an adventurous farmer willing to take a risk on an unproven crop. He grows specialty varieties for specific restaurants, such as shishito peppers for Slanted Door in San Francisco, and rare types of chard such as Ebette.

Ever since they started, Janet and Marty have farmed organically. "We really believe in organic," says Marty. "We never thought of doing it any other way. We farm *because* it is organic. It just seems like a very meaningful thing to do."

Janet has been a gardener all her life. "When Marty and I came to the point where we wanted to have our own business," she says, "it had to be a farm."

Kevin Lunny, a third-generation rancher, near the shoreline of Abbotts Lagoon in the Point Reyes National Seashore, where he raises grass-fed, certified organic beef.

And the name, Allstar Organics, how did that come about? "Well," says Janet, "we were trying to come up with a name, and we were stuck. Then one day when we were talking about it, our son, Bo, came walking up the drive wearing his red-white-and-blue, all-star baseball uniform. And there it was!"

Produce from Allstar Organics is found on the menus of numerous local restaurants, among them Slanted Door, MarketBar, Michael Mina, and Florio in San Francisco; Lark Creek Inn, Emporio Rulli, Comforts Café, Sol Food, and the Olema Inn in Marin County; and in produce markets like the famous Monterey Market in Berkeley, which has a simple philosophy: "to provide good fruits and vegetables in season."

Drakes Bay Family Farms

Kevin Lunny's grandfather had no intention of getting into ranching when he helped his brother-in-law get a loan for a dairy farm on the Point Reyes Peninsula. But when the in-law turned out to be a ne'er-do-well, Joe Lunny, a successful San Francisco steamship executive, took six months off and headed to Marin to see what he had inadvertently bought. Joe Lunny never returned to the city. Neither did his son, Joe Lunny, Jr. And neither did his grandson, Kevin.

Today, Drakes Bay Family Farms raises organic cattle on its fourteen hundred acres and, as the Historic G Ranch, is one of fifteen historic ranches and dairies operating within the boundaries of the Point Reyes National Seashore, remnants of the huge dairy farms that were established as far back as the 1850s.

Drakes Bay Family Farms produces the only certified organic beef in Marin County. The two hundred head of Hereford-Angus cows are raised in organic pastures bordering Drakes Estero, are fed organic feed before going to market, and are free of any growth hormones or other medicine used to ward off disease. The herd is closed. "We have not purchased a cow in thirty years," says Lunny. "Every animal is born and raised on this ranch."

The Lunny family's move from conventional to organic ranching began out of necessity. Like many small farmers and ranchers, the Lunnys were struggling. "The economics were getting tougher and tougher," says Lunny. "There wasn't enough income for our parents, much less my family." (He has triplets.) "It was a beautiful life, but it wasn't a living."

The family decided it needed to think differently. Lunny took over an adjacent oyster business, planted several acres of artichokes (which thrive in the cool, moist climate), and converted part of his beef herd to organic, seeing an opportunity to sell quality, not quantity.

"Surprisingly," says Lunny, "what started out as an economic driver turned out to be my deepest passion. What organic ranching does for the land, for biodiversity, and for the local market is amazing. It's awesome for a farmer to know who's enjoying our food. That's a blessing to us, because those people are actually paying more money for healthy food, and that directly supports us."

Drakes Bay Family Farms sells its organic beef through local farmers' markets and to nearby restaurants, such as the Drake's Beach Cafe. It can also be ordered directly from the ranch.

Peter Martinelli *(right)* in the field at Fresh Run Farm in Bolinas. The loamy soil in Paradise Valley is deep and rich.

Fresh Run Farm

If a young San Rafael man hadn't ridden his Indian motorcycle out to Bolinas one day in 1916 to fish for trout in Pine Gulch Creek, this tiny seaside town, home to artists, writers, and iconoclasts, might never have become the birthplace of Marin's organic farming movement.

But Jordan Martinelli returned to Pine Gulch Creek again and again, drawn to the freshwater that flows year-round against a rift in the notorious San Andreas Fault, and began buying land. Eventually, he owned five hundred acres in the aptly named Paradise Valley, where he set up a dairy operation.

That land, blessed with a cakey loam topsoil that runs twelve feet deep or more, still produces food, but today it's a cornucopia of organic produce brought from the ground by the hands of Peter Martinelli, the young trout fisherman's grandson.

Fresh Run Farm sits on 240 acres that stretch from shaded bottomland to contoured slopes to hillsides wooded with old groves of live oak. The farm ends on a ridge top that abuts the Point Reyes National Seashore and provides a view—on a fog-free day—clear across Marin County to the spires of downtown San Francisco.

Peter draws water from Pine Gulch Creek—which is still a steelhead trout run—to grow just about every type of row-crop vegetable, ranging from spring greens like lettuce and arugula to summer potatoes to fall squash and winter artichokes. "The only things I can't grow," he says, "are peppers and tomatoes. Not enough heat."

Rows of beets line a field at Fresh Run Farm.

Fresh Run Farm is located upstream from two of Marin's oldest organic farms, Paradise Valley Produce and Star Route Farms, both of which rely on water from Pine Gulch Creek.

On the Martinelli property, organic farming is still a family affair. Peter's sister-in-law, Susan Martinelli, has a house on the land and, under the label Creekside Garden, produces a variety of jams and jellies, dried fruit, vegetables such as okra and chayote, and Meyer lemons. Susan sells her wares at local farmers' markets. Produce from Fresh Run Farm can be found on the menu at the Olema Inn and Insalata's in Marin, Zuni Café and Quince in San Francisco, and Chez Panisse and Café Rouge in Berkeley.

Little Organic Farm

David Little went organic even before he became a farmer. "When I was ten," he says, "my parents let me have a pumpkin patch at the side of the house. It didn't take me long to realize that fish emulsion is better than some miracle product" when it comes to making things grow.

Today, David is a popular figure at the weekly farmers' markets in Marin County and San Francisco. It's hard to miss him. He's tall, gregarious, white-haired, and surrounded by boxes of organic potatoes grown on his farm near the town of Tomales, Marin's northernmost outpost on U.S. Highway 1.

David grows so many varieties of potato that his crop list reads like a United Nations' seating chart: Rose Finn Apple, Russian Banana, French, Yukon Gold, German Butterball, Yellow Finn, and Viking. And there's more: Ozette, Carola, Kennebec, Russet Norkotah, Mountain Rose, Charlotte, Lakatte, Red Thum, White Rose, and Katahdin.

David Little (right) harvesting dry-farmed potatoes at Little Organic Farm in Tomales. Workers (above) sort the potatoes, which are later sacked and stored in the cool darkness of Little's barn.

David dry farms his potatoes—as well as several varieties of cherry and heirloom tomatoes—in the rich sandy loam that is typical of northern Marin soil. Dry farming means that the crop is not irrigated during the season, but is instead nurtured by the moisture held in the soil (and the summer ocean fog). The result is a concentration of flavor, producing potatoes known for their taste and texture, and tomatoes so sweet they could be sold as candy. All in all, David has twenty-six acres under cultivation in several fields, including the potatoes, tomatoes, and a few other types of organic produce that he irrigates (squash, lettuce, onions, melons, and strawberries).

When he jumped into farming full time more than a dozen years ago, David knew organic was the way to go. "My marketing strategy was quality," he says. "Organic just made sense. Besides, I don't know how to do it any other way."

Winters in Marin are too wet for growing potatoes, but David still serves local shoppers and chefs from the stock of exotic spuds he stores in his well-weathered barn. There, in dozens and dozens of fifty-pound burlap bags, they wait in the cool darkness, a reminder of the passing seasons.

David's potatoes and other produce from Little Organic Farm can be found on the menus at such well-known San Francisco restaurants as Fifth Floor, Range, Greens, and MarketBar, as well as at Chez Panisse in Berkeley and the French Laundry in the Napa Valley.

Jesse Kuhn (right) studied sustainable agriculture in college and is one of Marin's youngest organic farmers. At Marin Roots Farm (above), he grows dozens of types of produce.

Marin Roots Farm

Perched on a ten-acre upland rise that straddles the Marin-Sonoma county line, Marin Roots Farm is located in an agricultural neighborhood that represents the entire cross-section of Marin's farm community.

Down below is the large Volpi Dairy, whose milking barn hums long into the night; next to it is the smaller Andante Dairy, producer of artisan goat's and cow's milk cheeses; to the west are the fields of County Line Harvest and La Tercera farms (the latter under the till of Annabelle Lenderink, sales manager for organic pioneer Star Route Farms); and across the highway to the south are the picturesque organic olive orchards of the McEvoy Ranch.

But when owner Jesse Kuhn first saw the land for his farm—which he found by putting a "farmland wanted" ad in the local newspaper—he wasn't thinking of the quality of his neighbors. He wanted good soil and enough water to grow all year. "I could tell the soil was good here," he says, "because the grass and the weeds were five feet tall."

Today, five years later, that overgrown field is brimming with rows of leafy greens, beets, fava beans, various types of tomatoes and multicolored carrots, broccoli rabe, chicory, chard, and berries.

Produce from Marin Roots Farm can be found on the menus of Boulette's Larder, Aziza, Nopa, MarketBar, and Foreign Cinema in San Francisco, and the Lark Creek Inn, Olema Inn, Cowgirl Cantina, Frantoio, Table, and Comforts Café in Marin.

⚜ Jesse Kuhn ⚜

Jesse Kuhn, at thirty-three, has come a long way in a short time. He founded Marin Roots Farm after studying sustainable agriculture in college, working first as a landscaper and then putting in apprentice time at other farms. The first season on the land was a rough one: maxed-out credit cards, repairs on the aging barn, fields of discarded debris ("I was always cutting buried barbed wire off the tiller").

Persistence, though, paid off and helped fulfill a longing he'd had since childhood for his own farm. "My grandmother had a green thumb," he says. "I have vivid memories of her farm in Nebraska, of visiting the farm and eating alfalfa fresh from the field. They really stuck in my mind."

Paradise Valley Produce

As the social turmoil of the sixties gave way to the New Age revolution of the seventies, many young people in search of community and a simpler rural life went "back to the land." Dennis Dierks, then a commercial artist, was one of them.

Eventually, though, the hard work and economic realities of farming drove most of the back-to-the-landers back to the city. Not Dennis. He stayed, outlasting the other members of a collective who in 1972 had bought fifty acres in Paradise Valley, a green wedge of land tucked between the San Andreas Fault and Pine Gulch Creek on the Bolinas peninsula, and became one of Marin's pioneering organic farmers.

Today, Dennis and his wife, Sandy, are still at it. They've raised five children on this rich bottomland, living in a beautiful home they built under the tall alders that drape over the creek and working the deep soil of Paradise Valley to produce fourteen varieties of organic lettuce; spinach, kale, and chard; several varieties of squash and potatoes; and an aromatic assortment of leeks and onions.

Dennis has always placed stewardship of the land foremost. "I didn't want to use chemicals," he says. "We were starting a family, and we wanted good, clean food."

Over the years, Dennis has "learned how to work with natural systems rather than against them" and has become a local expert in using natural means, such as capturing microbes from the air, to feed his soil.

Paradise Valley Produce in Bolinas is one of Marin's oldest organic farms, beginning as a collective in the 1970s. Fertile fields of deep loam host rows of lettuce, onion, and other produce *(left)*. Heirloom apple trees border the fields. Farm interns *(above)* clean freshly harvested leeks.

Sandy and Dennis Dierks of Paradise Valley Produce in Bolinas.

"We get our whole nutrient system within five miles of the farm," he says. "A farm can't be sustainable if you're trucking in stuff from all over. Our major focus is trying to create our own nutrient system."

Paradise Valley benefits from Pine Gulch Creek's year-round flow, a rarity in most parts of Marin, and Dennis's efforts to protect the annual steelhead trout runs in the creek earned his farm California's first certification as "salmon safe."

During the growing season, Dennis employs a number of young people as apprentices. They do field work, clean and box vegetables for market, and learn the techniques of growing organic food from a man who, after thirty years, says he's "still improving."

Dennis sells most of his crop through farmers' markets in Marin. "That's the best you can get," he says, "dealing directly with the people who are going to eat your food."

By the way, Paradise Valley's fourteen types of lettuce are Red Butter, Green Butter, Green Romaine, Red Romaine, Cocarde, Oscarde, Salad Bowl, French Crisp, Lollo, Freckles, Black-Seeded Simpson, Deer Tongue, Red Grand Rapids, and Green Grand Rapids.

Star Route Farms

Warren Weber has been called, at various points in his farming life, "the father of organic farming in California," one of the "Grand Old Men of Food," an "organic farming icon," and, most often, an "organic pioneer."

It's true that, as founder of the Star Route Farms, the oldest continually certified organic farm in California, Warren is deserving of all those labels. But, pluck them away and beyond the icon is a man who still likes to get his hands dirty doing what he loves: growing clean, healthy, tasty food in a way that connects the earth to the farmer and the farmer to the community.

That has been Warren's mission since 1974, when as a young former college professor he bought a plot of land alongside the Bolinas Lagoon, set up house in a train caboose, and started farming with a horse-drawn plow.

Organic from the first seed he planted, Warren at first sold to a scattering of local markets and health food stores, outposts of the fresh food revolution that was just beginning. The woman behind that revolution, Alice Waters, the founder of Chez Panisse restaurant in Berkeley, gave Star Route a big boost in the midseventies when she asked Warren to grow her signature mesclun salad mix for her.

Over the years, Warren acquired more land, and today Star Route has one hundred acres in Bolinas, forty of which are used for growing, and another plot of land in the Coachella Valley, where the warm winter

Warren Weber (left) stands in a field of greens at Star Route Farms, California's oldest continuously certified organic farm. In the fields (above), seedlings are ready for planting after being started in rows of greenhouses. When harvested, fresh-picked lettuces are put into boxes ready to be sold to customers throughout the Bay Area.

A row of trees bordering the fields at Star Route Farm in Bolinas, seen at sunset *(left)* and sunrise *(right)*.

allows the farm to grow food year-round. From these fields, Star Route produces an array of lettuces and a host of other leafy greens, seasonal vegetables of all types, and, in the greenhouse, edible flowers.

Well known among local chefs and close readers of menus, Star Route had its moment in the international spotlight during a 2005 visit to West Marin organic farms by Britain's Prince Charles and his wife, Camilla, the Duchess of Cornwall. After a chatty tour of the farmers' market in Point Reyes Station on Highway 1, where all the food is grown within twenty miles of the town, the royal couple dined with Warren and a group of other local farmers at Star Route.

Star Route sells through the Ferry Plaza Farmers' Market in San Francisco and Marin Civic Center farmers' markets, and it is common to see chefs at the farm's stand first thing in the morning, picking out produce for the evening or weekend menu.

Produce from Star Route is found in dozens of local restaurants, among them Chez Panisse, Zuni Café, Boulevard, Delfina, Jardinière, Slanted Door, Postrio, and Greens in San Francisco, and the Lark Creek Inn and Nick's Cove in Marin County.

Straus Family Creamery

Straus Family Creamery is a model of a modern organic dairy. For its first half-century, starting in 1941, when Bill and Ellen Straus began dairy farming in Marshall on the shores of Tomales Bay, the Straus farm was a conventional small dairy, selling its milk through cooperatives to larger producers.

By the 1990s, though, with milk prices falling and the industry shrinking, the family faced difficult financial choices. The future of their farm was at stake. Ellen Straus was already an environmental force in Marin County (as mentioned earlier, she was a founder of the Marin Agricultural Land Trust, a farmland preservation group formed in the 1970s to block urban development of West Marin), so when son Albert suggested the dairy become organic and make its own products, the family readily made the leap.

In 1994, the 660-acre farm became the first organic dairy west of the Mississippi River. Today, its three hundred Jersey-Holstein cows produce enough milk (about eight gallons each per day) for Straus to churn out not just its own brand of milk but also organic yogurt, ice cream, and butter, all products that are sold mostly to retail stores, but also to discriminating local restaurants such as Chez Panisse in Berkeley and the French Laundry in the Napa Valley. Straus sells its whole, reduced fat and nonfat milk in glass bottles in stores throughout California and in several other Western states (the whole milk comes with a layer of cream on top).

Albert Straus (above) manages the organic dairy operation at the Straus Family Creamery in Marshall. The family's ranch (left) stretches down to the shore of Tomales Bay.

Familiar scenes at the Straus Family Creamery *(above)*: an outbuilding on the farm; a cow returns to the barn after the afternoon milking; and fog on the hills above the ranch. Dairy cows graze on the farm's steep hillsides above Tomales Bay *(right)*.

Straus milk is also the basis for the nationally famous artisan cheeses made by Cowgirl Creamery of Point Reyes Station. The creamery, started in 1997 by former chefs Sue Conley (Bette's Oceanview Diner in Berkeley) and Peggy Smith (Chez Panisse), sells organic aged (Mt. Tam, Red Hawk) and fresh (fromage blanc, clabbered cottage) cheeses through its own stores in Point Reyes Station, the Ferry Building in San Francisco, and in Washington, D.C., as well as to local supermarkets and specialty stores (such as Rustic Bakery in Larkspur), and through its web site.

This type of marketing, which connects the farm directly to the end product, has helped Straus survive and keep alive Marin County's tradition of family farms. Straus continues to innovate, both in finding new ways to use its milk—like Barista Milk, made especially for espresso machines—and in developing sustainable farming practices.

Straus, for example, powers its dairy and the family home by turning manure from its cows into methane, saving as much as $6,000 a month in utility costs and preventing the methane from escaping into the atmosphere, where it would be damaging to the ozone layer. And last year, Straus became the first certified organic manufacturer in the nation to verify that all its products are uncontaminated by genetically modified organisms.

❧ Cowgirl Creamery ❧

Sue Conley (the former owner of Bette's Oceanview Diner in Berkeley) and Peggy Smith (formerly of Chez Panisse) teamed up in Point Reyes Station to make a variety of artisan cheeses from the organic milk produced by the Straus Family Creamery of West Marin. Cowgirl Creamery quickly became known for its triple-cream Mt. Tam, clabbered cottage cheese, fromage blanc, and crème fraîche.

About the Recipes

The recipes in *Organic Marin: Recipes from Land to Table* come from restaurants around the San Francisco Bay Area that support local organic farmers and ranchers by buying their produce, meat, and dairy products. Each of the delicious recipes contributed by these restaurants uses one or more of the seasonal organic ingredients that are grown in Marin.

Besides providing four seasons' worth of recipes based on the organic bounty of Marin, we hope this book also creates a bit of inspiration. Small farmers and ranchers depend on direct public support to survive, and there is no better way to demonstrate your support than by shopping whenever possible at local farmers' markets.

These markets, common in Marin, San Francisco, and throughout the Bay Area, are becoming an increasing part of the food landscape in other regions of the country. For a buyer, the markets are an assured source of fresh, local organic food, typically grown within one hundred miles, or closer, of the market. They also are an opportunity to meet the person who plants, grows, and harvests that food—the connection between food and community that young Mickey Murch, the Bolinas farmer, talks about in the introduction.

For the farmers, the markets provide a chance to be paid more for their wares than they would receive from a regional food distributor or a supermarket chain. That extra money might make the difference between just breaking even for the season and turning a profit. But the one-on-one interaction between the farmer and the consumer—the link between land and table—is also a major attraction for growers. To repeat a quote from Dennis Dierks of Paradise Valley: "That's the best you can get, dealing directly with the people who are going to eat your food."

spring

Baby radishes, just out of the soil at Star Route Farms, are cleaned before being sent to a local restaurant *(right)*.

In the spring, at the end of the day, you should smell like dirt.
— Margaret Atwood

spring

There's nothing shy about spring in Marin County. For this season of renewal and growth, a simple arrival won't do. Instead, spring in Marin promenades in grand style across the hills, valleys, and seaside bluffs, accompanied by an entourage of living color.

First on the scene are the bright green shoots of new grass, rich with chlorophyll and rain-fed from the winter. They rise delicately in the low meadows, a carpet amid the brown detritus of the previous year.

Then come the flowers: pink shooting stars on rocky slopes, tiny white milkmaids on the hills, and the aptly named footsteps-of-spring in the fields. The flora build in volume and crescendo as the days lengthen and warm, ranging from the delicate blues, whites, and lavenders of the Douglas iris to the yellow fields of buttercups. By the time the bursting orange of the California poppy appears, spring is in full swing.

For the organic farmers and ranchers of West Marin, this time of year offers every advantage. Creeks are brimming, farm ponds are full, and the soil is still moist from winter, perfect for nurturing new crops. Helped on by lingering spring showers, tall, sweet grass covers the hillsides, natural forage for herds of beef and dairy cows.

Some farmers are harvesting winter fields of leafy lettuces and other greens, baby beets, fava beans, carrots, fresh herbs, and the last of the artichokes. Spring is a prime laying season for hens, and fresh

organic eggs abound. Strawberries begin their march toward summer, and local blueberries appear—and disappear—in a few weeks.

Spring is a time of rebirth and promise. But these are also days of completion and fulfillment, a time to reap the first harvest of the year, a time to celebrate the respite from the colder months just gone by and enjoy the fruits (and vegetables) of winter's labors. Here, thanks to the bounty of the land and the dedication of Marin's organic farmers and ranchers, spring is Nature's way of saying: "Let's eat!"

Workers at Star Route Farms harvest spring lettuce *(left and above)*.
Colorful baby beets *(above, right)* are a favorite spring crop at
Fresh Run Farms.

Fava Bean Bruschetta

MarketBar, San Francisco

This tapas-style appetizer is a simple and delicious start to a spring meal. MarketBar uses Marin Star Route Farm's young, tender fava beans. Because of the simplicity of this dish, use a good-quality sea salt and extra-virgin olive oil.

1 pound fava beans, shelled

1 clove garlic, minced

1 tablespoon freshly squeezed lemon juice

1/2 tablespoon minced fresh thyme

1/4 cup extra-virgin olive oil, plus 2 tablespoons

1/2 teaspoon sea salt, plus more for sprinkling

1/4 teaspoon freshly ground pepper

1 sweet or sourdough baguette

Bring a large saucepan of salted water to a boil over high heat. Blanch the fava beans for 5 minutes, then drain and plunge into an ice-water bath. Once the beans are cool, peel them by pinching off the skin.

Put the beans in a food processor. Add the garlic, lemon juice, and thyme and pulse for several seconds until the beans are coarsely chopped. With the machine running, add the 1/4 cup olive oil until well combined. Stir in the 1/2 teaspoon salt and the pepper. Set aside.

Preheat an oven to 350°F. Cut the baguette into 1/4-inch diagonal slices. Using a pastry brush, coat both sides of the bread slices with the 2 tablespoons olive oil. Place the bread in a single layer on a baking sheet and toast in the oven for 10 to 15 minutes, until light golden brown. Remove from the oven and let cool for 5 minutes. Using a butter knife, spread 1 teaspoon fava bean puree on each toast. Sprinkle lightly with sea salt and serve at room temperature.

Makes 30 to 35 bruschetta

❧ Peeling Fava Beans ❧

Fava beans, also called broad beans, have been cultivated in Southwest Asia and the Mediterranean for thousands of years. The beans are eaten fresh when picked early in the season, or as a dried bean when allowed to mature on the vine. To cook fresh favas, shell the beans from the spongy pods. Bring a large pot of salted water to a boil and blanch the favas for 3 minutes. Drain the beans and refresh with cold water. Peel the beans by pinching the dark green ridge on the round side of the bean and pulling open the skin. Slip out the bright green bean and discard the skin. One pound of fava bean pods will yield 1 cup of shelled beans.

⚘ Reconstituting Dried ⚘ Mushrooms

Dried mushrooms are reconstituted to restore the soft texture of the fresh food. To reconstitute dried mushrooms, soak them in a small bowl of hot water or broth for 20 to 30 minutes and keep the mushrooms submerged with a plate. Once the mushrooms are softened, they may be drained, squeezed of excess liquid, chopped or sliced, and added to a dish. They provide a rich flavor that will significantly enhance the taste of other foods, sauces, and soups.

Roasted Wild Mushroom Soup with Crème Fraîche

AVA Restaurant, San Anselmo

AVA uses the freshest local wild mushrooms for this hearty soup. White domestic mushrooms may be substituted if the wild ones are not available.
In that case, add a few reconstituted dried porcini to enrich the flavor of the dish.

3 tablespoons olive oil
4 tablespoons unsalted butter
2 pounds cremini mushrooms, chopped
1 pound mixed wild mushrooms (chanterelles, morels, and porcini)
½ teaspoon salt
¼ teaspoon freshly ground pepper
1 yellow onion, diced
2 cloves garlic, minced
1 tablespoon minced fresh thyme
½ cup dry white wine
6 cups vegetable stock
3 tablespoons crème fraîche

Heat a Dutch oven or heavy stockpot over high heat until almost smoking. Quickly add 2 tablespoons of the oil, 3 tablespoons of the butter, and the mushrooms to the pan. Decrease the heat to medium, add the salt and pepper, and sauté the mushrooms until the juices are released and nearly evaporated, about 10 minutes.

Heat a separate medium sauté pan over medium heat and add the remaining 1 tablespoon olive oil and 1 tablespoon butter. Sauté the onion for 10 minutes, or until it begins to brown. Add the garlic and thyme and sauté for 2 minutes. Add the white wine and cook for about 5 minutes, or until reduced completely. Transfer the onion mixture to the mushrooms and cook for about 10 minutes, or until well browned.

Stir the vegetable stock into the mushroom mixture and simmer over medium-low heat for 10 minutes. Coarsely blend the soup in a food processor or with a hand-held blender. Return the soup to the pot if needed and reheat over low heat. Taste and adjust the seasoning. Spoon the soup into warmed bowls and garnish each with 1 teaspoon or so of crème fraîche.

Serves 4 to 6 as a first course

Serrano Ham, Pears, and Haricot Vert Salad with Valdeón Cheese

Insalata's, San Anselmo

This is an all-season recipe. In the spring, Insalata's serves this composed salad with ripe Bosc pears, while in the fall it might use figs or persimmons. Organic arugula or escarole is a great substitute for the frisée, and gorgonzola may be substituted for the Valdeón.

Valdeón Cream

½ cup Valdeón cheese

½ cup heavy cream

¼ teaspoon salt

⅛ teaspoon freshly ground pepper

Sherry Vinaigrette

1 teaspoon minced shallot

2 tablespoons sherry vinegar

⅛ teaspoon kosher salt

1 teaspoons honey

½ teaspoon Dijon mustard

2 tablespoons hazelnut oil

2 tablespoons extra-virgin olive oil

8 paper-thin slices serrano ham or prosciutto

8 ounces haricots verts, trimmed and blanched for 3 minutes

2 firm, ripe Bosc pears, peeled, cored, and thinly sliced

Leaves from 1 small head frisée lettuce

½ cup chopped Marcona almonds

For the Valdeón cream: Combine the cheese and cream in a blender or food processor. Blend until just smooth. Stir in the salt and pepper. Transfer the cream to a squeeze bottle. Refrigerate until ready to use.

For the sherry vinaigrette: Combine the shallot, vinegar, and salt in a small bowl and let stand for 5 minutes. Whisk in the honey, mustard, and oils. Taste and adjust the seasoning.

Assemble the salad by placing 2 slices of ham on each of 4 plates. In a medium nonaluminum bowl, combine the blanched haricots verts, pear slices, frisée leaves, almonds, and ¼ cup of the vinaigrette. Toss gently and mound on top of the ham. Drizzle with the Valdeón cream and serve immediately.

Serves 4 as a first course

☙ Insalata's ❧

Vegetarians and carnivores alike flock to San Anselmo's Insalata's. The restaurant's Mediterranean and Middle Eastern–inspired menu features classics like hummus with warm pita and spicy grilled chicken marinated in organic yogurt. Time-strapped locals wanting gourmet dinners on the fly head to the restaurant's takeout section for foods like whole roast chicken stuffed with citrus and rosemary and organic blanched beets. Insalata's uses free-range chicken from local ranches and organic produce from Marin growers such as Star Route Farms and Fresh Run Farm.

ꙮ Making Potato ꙮ Gnocchi

Gnocchi, or dumplings, are made throughout Italy from a variety of ingredients, including bread crumbs, semolina, and ricotta cheese. Potato gnocchi are a beloved Roman specialty, and making them takes practice, patience, and persistence. At their best, these petite dumplings are light and delicate. To ensure a lighter dumpling, use a potato ricer to mash the potatoes and mix the dough by hand. Gnocchi may be served with almost any favorite sauce and can be served as a first course or a main course.

Gnocchi with Morels and Peas

Marché aux Fleurs, Ross

Marché aux Fleurs highlights spring mushrooms and fresh peas in this light gnocchi dish. Other wild mushrooms, such as chanterelles or black trumpets, may be used if morels are not available. To make the gnocchi ahead, freeze them on a baking sheet, then package them in a heavy-duty plastic freezer bag.

Gnocchi

2 pounds russet potatoes

2 1/2 cups all-purpose flour

1 tablespoon kosher salt

1 large egg

Sauce

1 1/2 pounds morels, soaked to remove dirt and patted dry (rinsed chanterelles may be substituted)

2 tablespoons unsalted butter

1/2 teaspoon kosher salt

1/2 cup heavy cream

8 ounces green peas, shelled and blanched for 1 minute

1 tablespoon freshly squeezed lemon juice

1/4 teaspoon freshly ground pepper

1 tablespoon truffle oil for garnish

For the gnocchi: Preheat an oven to 350°F and bake the potatoes for about 1 hour, or until tender when pierced with a knife. While the potatoes are still hot, use a large spoon to scoop out the flesh and press it through a potato ricer into a large bowl. Add the flour and salt to the potatoes, using a pastry cutter to mix the ingredients together. Stir the egg into the potato mixture until blended. Add flour 1 tablespoon at a time if needed, to make a slightly firm, nonsticky dough. The less flour you use, the lighter the gnocchi will be.

Divide the dough into 8 pieces. On a lightly floured work surface, roll each piece into a rope about 1/2 inch thick. Add more flour if needed to keep the dough from sticking. Gently press the back of a fork into the dough at 1-inch intervals. Using a knife, cut the gnocchi into 1-inch diagonal sections. Repeat with the remaining dough.

For the sauce: Cut the morels into 2-inch pieces. Melt the butter in a large saucepan over high heat and add the mushrooms and 1/4 teaspoon of the salt. Sauté for 3 to 5 minutes, until the mushrooms release their juices.

(continued on next page)

Gnocchi with Morels and Peas
(continued)

Decrease the heat to medium-low and stir in the cream and peas. Simmer for about 2 minutes, or until the sauce thickens. Add the lemon juice, the remaining ¼ teaspoon salt, and the pepper. Set aside and keep warm.

Cook half of the gnocchi in a large pot of salted boiling water for about 2 minutes, or until they rise to the top. Using a slotted spoon, gently transfer the gnocchi with a slotted spoon to 2 or 3 shallow bowls. Place the bowls in a low oven. Repeat with the remaining gnocchi. Spoon the warm sauce over the gnocchi and drizzle each serving with a little truffle oil. Serve immediately.

Serves 4 to 6 as a main course

Olive Oil–Poached Halibut with Salsa Verde

AVA Restaurant, San Anselmo

Cooking fish fillets at a very low temperature in olive oil keeps the fish moist and is a great alternative to poaching in broth. Salmon and sea bass also fare well with this style of preparation. Allow 2 hours for preparing the poaching oil.

Poaching Oil

4 cups extra-virgin olive oil

2 sprigs rosemary

3 sprigs thyme

2 cloves garlic

1 shallot, halved

4 (6-ounce, 1-inch-thick) halibut fillets

¼ teaspoon kosher salt

⅛ teaspoon freshly ground pepper

Salsa Verde

½ bunch flat-leaf parsley, stemmed
    and minced

1 shallot, minced

2 tablespoon capers, rinsed

2 tablespoons Champagne vinegar

¼ cup extra-virgin olive oil

⅛ teaspoon kosher salt

⅛ teaspoon freshly ground pepper

Vinaigrette

1 tablespoon freshly squeezed
    lemon juice

3 tablespoons extra-virgin olive oil

⅛ teaspoon kosher salt

Pinch of freshly ground pepper

1 fennel bulb, thinly sliced, fronds reserved

1 bunch radishes, trimmed and thinly sliced

For the poaching oil: Combine all the ingredients in a large saucepan. Heat the oil over low heat to 150°F or to a bare simmer. Maintain at this temperature for 2 hours. Strain the oil and set aside at room temperature.

Season the halibut fillets with the salt and pepper and let stand for 30 minutes. Heat the poaching oil in a nonstick large sauté pan to a low simmer over medium-low heat. Carefully add the fillets and poach the fish for 20 to 30 minutes, until slightly firm to the touch.

For the salsa verde: Combine all the ingredients in a medium bowl. Taste and adjust the seasoning.

To serve, remove the fish from the hot oil using a slotted metal spatula and blot on paper towels. For the vinaigrette: Whisk all the ingredients together in a small bowl. Dress the fennel and radishes and mound on each of 4 plates. Place a fillet on top of each mound and garnish with 1 tablespoon of the salsa verde and fennel fronds.

Serves 4 as a main course

ꞔ McEvoy Olive Oil ꞔ

Nan McEvoy once worked for a company that bought ink by the barrel. Today, she sells organic olive oil by the bottle. The granddaughter of the founder of the *San Francisco Chronicle* newspaper, McEvoy did a stint as a reporter there and eventually headed the company's board of directors. Looking for a place to retire, she bought a 550-acre former dairy farm in northern Marin and planted it with one hundred olive trees. Today, McEvoy Ranch has eighteen thousand trees and produces everything from premium olive oil to honey, all in an ecologically sustaining environment. McEvoy olive oil is unfiltered and made without any chemical processing. The ranch is a member of the California Certified Organic Farmers.

Fish

Sustainable seafood, local organic produce, and close-enough-to-get-splashed views of Richardson Bay are just a few reasons locals and visitors flock to this Sausalito seafood market and eatery. Order from the regular menu or choose one of their daily specials. Depending on the season, that might be a fully loaded BLT with guacamole, heirloom tomato slices, and a generous piece of halibut, or crab Louis, delicate fresh crabmeat piled atop crisp, locally grown organic lettuce.

Green Goddess Salmon and Watercress Salad

Fish, Sausalito

Fish highlights local salmon in this flavorful Marin Roots Farm watercress salad with an updated green goddess dressing. The salmon for this simple salad can also be grilled or poached.

Dressing

3 anchovy fillets, rinsed

2 cloves garlic

1 cup firmly packed fresh flat-leaf parsley leaves, blanched for 5 seconds, drained and squeezed dry

2 tablespoons olive oil

2 tablespoons minced green onion (including green parts)

1 tablespoon minced fresh tarragon

½ cup good-quality mayonnaise

2 tablespoons freshly squeezed lemon juice

1 tablespoon red wine vinegar

⅛ teaspoon freshly ground pepper

1½ pounds local king salmon fillets, pin bones removed

¼ teaspoon kosher salt

⅛ teaspoon freshly ground pepper

2 tablespoons olive oil

8 ounces watercress, stemmed

4 lemon wedges

For the dressing: Puree the anchovies, garlic, parsley, and olive oil in a blender or mini food processor until smooth. Scrape into a medium bowl. Stir in the remaining dressing ingredients and mix well. Taste and adjust the seasoning. Cover and refrigerate until ready to serve.

Heat a large nonstick sauté pan over high heat until hot. Season the salmon with the salt and pepper. Add the oil to the pan and sear the fillets, skin side down, for 3 to 4 minutes, until golden brown and crisp. Repeat on the other side. Remove from the pan and let rest for 5 minutes. Gently flake the salmon into a bowl with a fork.

To assemble the salad, mound the watercress on a platter or 4 plates and strew the salmon on top. Drizzle the dressing over the salad and garnish with lemon wedges. Serve chilled or at room temperature.

Serves 4 as a main course

Lamb and Apricot Stew

Lark Creek Inn, Larkspur

The kitchen at Lark Creek Inn creates an incredibly tender lamb stew by searing and then braising leg of lamb with seasonal apricots. The leg of lamb may be roasted the day before, and dried apricots may be used as an alternative if fresh ones are not in season.

5 tablespoons olive oil

1 (3- to 4-pound) leg of lamb, bone out and cut into 2-inch cubes

1 tablespoon minced fresh rosemary

4 cloves garlic

1 teaspoon salt

4 anchovy fillets

2 large yellow onions, chopped

⅛ teaspoon red pepper flakes

6 cups dry red wine

1 bay leaf

8 fresh apricots, halved and pitted

Heat a large Dutch oven or heavy ovenproof sauté pan over medium-high heat, add 2 tablespoons of olive oil, and sear 8 to 10 cubes of lamb in a single layer until lightly browned on both sides, 12 to 15 minutes. Transfer the seared meat to a plate and sear the remaining lamb.

For the seasoning, use a mortar and pestle or mini-food processor to grind the rosemary, garlic, salt, anchovies, and 3 tablespoons olive oil into a coarse paste.

Preheat an oven to 275°F. Once all the lamb is seared, reheat the same Dutch oven over medium heat (do not wash the pan). Add the onions and sauté for about 10 minutes, or until tender. Stir in the rosemary-anchovy mixture and red pepper flakes and sauté for 2 minutes. Add the wine and simmer for 30 to 35 minutes, until reduced by half. Add water to the pan until the meat is barely covered and stir in the bay leaf. Bring the stew to a low boil and add the apricots. Cover the pan with a tight lid. Roast in the oven for about 2 hours, or until the lamb is tender. The apricots will disintegrate and thicken the sauce. Remove from the oven. Taste and adjust the seasoning.

Serves 4 to 6 as a main course

❦ Lark Creek Inn ❦

Set in an ancient redwood grove on Magnolia Avenue in the town of Larkspur, the Lark Creek Inn has been winning the hearts of diners and critics alike since opening in 1989. In contrast to the dark-wooded bar greeting guests at the entrance, the dining area is flooded with natural light during the day and candlelit by night. It is a perennial special-occasion spot and is best known for inventive country cooking using mostly organic ingredients from local farmers and ranchers.

Just off the western stretch of Chestnut Street in San Francisco, a district famous for its young urban clientele, Lettüs is an oasis of organic foods. Customers can dine on locally sourced menu items such as vegan fresh spring rolls, mango chicken lettuce cups, and spicy red Thai curry.

Vegetables on Quinoa with Miso-Ginger Sauce

Lettüs Café Organic, San Francisco

This Bay Area organic café serves tasty one-dish meals that are loaded with fresh local vegetables and whole grains. This recipe may also be made with brown rice.

Sauce

1½ cups vegetable stock or water
½ cup white miso
3 tablespoons freshly squeezed lemon juice
1 tablespoon light soy sauce
1 tablespoon toasted sesame oil
1 tablespoon agave nectar
⅛ teaspoon chili paste (optional)
1 tablespoon canola oil
½ cup finely chopped red onion
2 tablespoons grated fresh ginger
1 teaspoon minced garlic

Quinoa

3 cups vegetable stock
¼ teaspoon sea salt
2 cups quinoa

1 cup julienned carrots
1 cup broccoli florets
1 cup green beans or asparagus, cut into 2-inch pieces
2 tablespoons canola oil
1 cup thinly sliced red bell pepper

3 ounces shiitake mushrooms, stemmed and sliced
1½ cups cubed baked tofu or cooked chicken breast
1 cup corn
Leaves from 6 cilantro and basil sprigs, chopped

For the sauce: Combine the stock, miso, lemon juice, soy sauce, sesame oil, agave nectar, and chili paste in a small bowl and mix well. Heat the canola oil in a small saucepan over medium heat. Sauté the onion, ginger, and garlic for about 2 minutes, or until fragrant. Stir in the miso mixture and bring to a low boil. Remove from the heat and set aside until ready to serve.

For the quinoa: Bring the vegetable stock and salt to a boil in a large saucepan. Stir in the quinoa and return to a boil. Decrease the heat to a simmer, cover, and cook for 15 minutes, until all the liquid is absorbed. Remove from the heat and let stand, covered.

(continued on next page)

Vegetables on Quinoa with Miso-Ginger Sauce
(continued)

In a large pot of salted boiling water, blanch the carrots, broccoli, and green beans for 3 minutes. Drain and plunge into ice water. Drain again and pat the vegetables dry. Heat a large sauté pan over high heat, add 2 tablespoons of oil, and sauté the pepper and mushrooms for 2 minutes, or until the pepper is crisp-tender. Add the tofu and sauté until lightly browned, about 5 minutes. Stir in the blanched vegetables and corn and stir-fry for 5 minutes, until everything is heated through. Taste and adjust the seasoning.

To serve, fluff the quinoa with a fork and divide it among shallow soup bowls. Top with the sautéed vegetables and spoon a heaping tablespoon of warm miso-ginger sauce over each serving. Sprinkle with the cilantro and basil.

Serves 4 to 6 as a main course

Panna Cotta with Fresh Strawberries

Scott Howard, San Francisco

This simple panna cotta recipe has a wonderful finish with fleur de sel and good-quality olive oil. Chef Howard substitutes fresh local fruits to complement the creamy texture. Try ripe cherries in summer and lightly sautéed apples in winter.

1 package plain gelatin

2 tablespoons cold water

1½ cups heavy cream

1 vanilla bean, halved lengthwise, or 1 teaspoon vanilla extract

½ cup sugar

2 cups buttermilk

1 tablespoon extra-virgin olive oil

½ teaspoon fleur de sel

1 pint ripe strawberries, hulled and quartered

Sprinkle the gelatin over the water in a small bowl and let stand for 5 minutes. Combine the cream and vanilla bean, if using, in a large saucepan and bring to a boil over medium heat. Decrease the heat to low and add the sugar. Stir until the sugar dissolves, then stir in the gelatin mixture until dissolved. Stir in the buttermilk and remove from the heat. Remove the vanilla bean and scrape the seeds into the pan. If using the vanilla extract, stir it in now. Strain the mixture through a fine-meshed sieve into 6 (4-ounce) ramekins. Let cool to room temperature, then cover and refrigerate for about 4 hours, or until set.

To serve, run a knife around the insides of the ramekins to loosen the panna cotta. Invert the ramekins on a serving plate and gently slide the panna cottas out. Drizzle each with ½ teaspoon olive oil and a pinch of fleur de sel. Top with the strawberries and serve.

Serves 6

⟶ Raspberry Coulis ⟵

This simple sauce tastes of fresh berries and complements the smoothness of panna cotta.

1 pint fresh raspberries (blueberries, black-berries, or strawberries may be substituted)

2 tablespoons water

¼ cup granulated sugar

Pinch of salt

1 teaspoon fresh lemon juice

Combine the raspberries, water, sugar, and salt in a medium nonaluminum saucepan. Bring to a simmer over medium heat. Cook, stirring, until the sugar is dissolved and the berries are heated through, about 2 minutes. Transfer to a blender or food processor and puree until smooth.

Strain through a fine-meshed sieve into a small bowl, pressing the solids with the back of a large spoon. Discard the seeds and stir the lemon juice into the puree. Cover and re-frigerate for at least 2 hours or up to 4 days.

Meyer Lemon Sorbet

Table Café, Larkspur

Refreshing sorbet is a perfect light dessert for warm weather meals. Other citrus fruits, such as grapefruits, limes, blood oranges, or a combination, are excellent substitutes. Make extra sugar syrup and store it in the refrigerator to use it as a base for other fruit sorbets.

✑ Meyer Lemons ✑

A favorite of chefs and gourmets, the Meyer lemon is rounder than a regular lemon and has a thin, smooth skin. The fruit is bright yellow, often with a slight orange tint when ripe. Sweeter and less acidic in flavor than a common lemon, it is popular for use in desserts. The flavor is a cross between a lemon and a tangerine. Meyer lemon trees produce fruit from fall through spring and are common throughout northern California.

1 cup sugar

1 cup water

Zest stripped from 1 Meyer lemon

3 mint sprigs

2¼ cups freshly squeezed Meyer lemon juice

¼ cup freshly squeezed lime juice

Pinch of kosher salt

Combine the sugar, water, lemon zest, and mint in a large saucepan and stir over medium-low heat until the sugar dissolves. Simmer for 10 minutes and then strain into a large bowl. Discard the mint and let the mixture cool to room temperature.

Stir the lemon juice, lime juice, and salt into the syrup. Cover and refrigerate for at least 2 hours. Freeze in an ice cream maker according to the manufacturer's instructions. Serve immediately, or pack into a container and freeze for 2 to 3 hours. Let stand at room temperature to soften slightly before serving if frozen solid.

Serves 6

ORGANIC
Roma Tomatoes
$ 1.95 Lb.

summer

By late summer, after months without rain, the pastureland of West Marin (seen here in Nicasio) turns deep brown and needs only a dose of warm afternoon sun to become a golden backdrop *(left)*.

Eat what's locally available. Eat with your family and friends.
Buy from a nearby market. Eat what's exactly in season.
—Alice Waters

summer

In contrast to spring in Marin, summer is indeed a shy season. It first appears tentatively, a few warm days here, a few more there—and usually in the inland valleys. On the coastal ridges and bottomland near the ocean, where most of Marin's organic farms and ranches are, the fog persists, keeping the days cool and the hillsides green.

Little by little, though, the land dries, the green fades, and the signature summer palette of West Marin appears: golden hills of dried grass, leafy green groves of live oak or bay laurel, and cloudless skies dimmed only by the perennial brackets of night and morning fog.

Marin County, like all of northern California, has a Mediterranean climate. There is no summer rain, so farmers must either irrigate their land or coax their crops out of dry soil. Some, like Star Route Farms or Paradise Valley Produce in Bolinas, depend on local creeks for water. Others, like Marin Roots Farm near Nicasio, draw from ponds filled with runoff rainwater. And a few, like Little Organic Farm in Tomales, by necessity or choice, dry farm, using the damp clay of their land to nourish rows of heirloom potatoes and tomatoes.

In summer, the bounty of Marin overflows at local farmers' markets. Tomatoes—Early Girls, cherries, and heirlooms with names like Green Zebra, Brandywine Red, and Yellow Ruffles—glow in the sun. Equally colorful boxes of sweet peppers and hot chilies demand the eye. Aromatic displays of blackberries,

raspberries, and strawberries invite passersby for a taste. And the baskets of greens explode with mesclun, arugula, mâche, and lettuces of every stripe.

As summer progresses and the days warm (yes, even on the coast), in come the melons, the bulbous eggplants and their more petite Asian cousins, and the summer squashes.

At summer's end, due to the quirks of the Marin climate, the temperatures peak, and farmers push their fields to capacity, hoping for one more crop before the autumn rains. For local restaurants and shoppers, this is prime time, when the best of the summer fruit and vegetables are found along with the first tastes of fall.

Colorful cherry tomatoes (as well as heirlooms) and eggplants abound at Marin farmers' markets during the summer.

Crab Deviled Eggs

MarketBar, San Francisco

*Fresh local crab and spinach make this decadent twist on
a classic party dish a favorite at the MarketBar in San Francisco. The eggs can be
made the day before and served as an appetizer.*

6 large eggs

2 cups packed spinach leaves,
well rinsed

4 ounces fresh lump crabmeat,
picked over for shell

¼ cup good-quality mayonnaise

1 tablespoon white wine vinegar

1 clove garlic, minced

½ teaspoon sugar

¼ teaspoon salt

¼ teaspoon freshly ground
pepper

Put the eggs in a saucepan and add cold water to cover.
Bring to a boil, remove from the heat, cover, and let
stand for 15 minutes. Drain and peel the eggs. Let cool.

Place the wet spinach in a small sauté pan and sauté
over medium heat until wilted. Put the spinach in a tea
towel and wring out all the water. Finely chop the
spinach.

Cut the eggs in half lengthwise and carefully remove the
yolks, reserving the whites. Mash the yolks in a medium
bowl with a fork. Add all the remaining ingredients
and mix well. Taste and adjust the seasoning. Spoon
1 heaping teaspoon of egg yolk into each egg white
half. Refrigerate until ready to serve.

Makes 12 deviled eggs

⚜ Clark Summit Ranch ⚜

A few years ago, Liz Cunninghame and
Dan Bagley had a few free-range chickens
on their 160-acre Clark Summit Ranch in
Tomales. They loved the taste of the eggs,
and so did their friends. Today, Clark Summit
Ranch has two thousand Americana, Rhode
Island Red, Barred Rock, and other laying
hens that produce nine hundred to one thousand organic eggs a day. The hens thrive on
a diet of organic grain, organic whey from
Cowgirl Creamery, and, being free-range,
local bugs and weeds. Clark Summit sells
through local farmers' markets and grocers
and directly from the ranch.

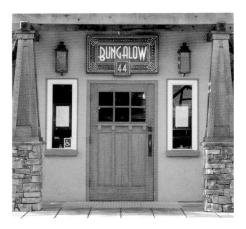

Heirloom Tomato Flat Bread

Bungalow 44, Mill Valley

Bungalow 44 serves flat breads that reflect each season's best ingredients. This recipe shows off the bounty of summer, with ripe tomatoes and fragrant basil. The dough may be made ahead of time and kept refrigerated for up to 2 days.

ꞈ Bungalow 44 ꞈ

Tucked into downtown Mill Valley, Bungalow 44 draws in locals with friendly service and dining options to suit any mood. The restaurant's main area is modern and lively, with an open kitchen and a popular bar where locals meet for specialty cocktails. The adjoining room is better suited for a quiet dinner, with a fire during the winter and removable panels that allow for a breeze during warmer weather. Like its sister restaurant, Buckeye Roadhouse, Bungalow 44 offers such homey favorites as fried chicken, Parmesan truffle fries, and a mean burger. For a lighter dish, try the chopped Chicken "44": an anything-but-boring salad featuring avocado, pine nuts, and jalapeno-tomatillo vinaigrette.

Dough
1¼ cups all-purpose flour
⅛ teaspoon baking powder
½ teaspoon sea salt
½ cup warm water
3 tablespoons extra-virgin olive oil

Basil Oil
½ cup firmly packed fresh basil leaves
⅓ cup extra-virgin olive oil

Fried Garlic
½ cup canola oil
6 cloves garlic, thinly sliced

½ cup grated Parmesan cheese
½ cup shredded mozzarella cheese
3 heirloom tomatoes, thinly sliced
Sea salt and freshly ground pepper
⅓ cup shaved pecorino romano cheese
Minced fresh basil for garnish

For the dough: Combine the flour, baking powder, and salt in a large bowl. Stir with a whisk to blend. Combine the water and oil in a cup and stir into the dry ingredients. Transfer the dough to a floured work surface and knead until smooth, about 5 minutes. Divide the dough in half, cover with a damp towel, and let the dough rest for 30 minutes.

For the basil oil: Blanch the basil in boiling water for 10 seconds, then drain and plunge into ice water to cool. Squeeze dry and place in a blender with the extra-virgin olive oil. Blend for 20 seconds and pass through a fine-meshed sieve; discard the solids.

For the fried garlic: Heat the canola oil in a small saucepan over medium-high heat to 325°F. Fry the garlic slices until just golden brown, 2 to 3 seconds. Drain in a fine-meshed sieve, then transfer the garlic to a paper towel to soak up excess oil.

Preheat an oven to 400°F with a pizza stone inside, if you have one. Flatten each dough ball into a disk and

(continued on next page)

Heirloom Tomato Flat Bread

(continued)

roll into an 8-inch round. Place the rounds directly on the pizza stone. If not using a pizza stone, place the rounds on a baking sheet. Prick the dough all over with a fork and bake for 10 to 12 minutes, or until just golden. Remove from the oven and increase the oven temperature to 425°F.

Sprinkle half of the Parmesan and mozzarella on each baked bread. Place the breads in the oven on the pizza stone or baking sheet and bake for 10 minutes, until the cheese melts and just starts to brown. Remove from the oven and layer each with the tomato slices in a single layer, season with salt and pepper, and drizzle evenly with the basil oil. Top each with half of the pecorino cheese shavings and return to the oven for about 5 minutes, or until the pecorino turns slightly golden. Remove from the oven and garnish with basil and fried garlic. Use a pizza wheel to cut each bread into 6 slices and serve right away.

Serves 4 as a first course

Mozzarella, Tomato, and Basil Salad

Poggio, Sausalito

Originating on the island of Capri in the 1950s, the caprese salad has evolved into a classic summer dish using the freshest ingredients. The chefs at Poggio make fresh mozzarella by hand daily for their customers.

3 tablespoons aged balsamic vinegar

¼ teaspoon sea salt, plus more for sprinkling

⅓ cup extra-virgin olive oil

⅛ teaspoon freshly ground pepper

1 pound fresh mozzarella, cut into ¼-inch slices

2 pounds ripe tomatoes, cut into ¼-inch slices

¼ cup firmly packed fresh basil leaves

Combine the vinegar and the ¼ teaspoon salt in a small bowl. Whisk in the olive oil and pepper.

On each of 4 salad plates, create a tower of the mozzarella, tomatoes, and basil, starting with a tomato slice, followed by a mozzarella slice and 2 basil leaves. Repeat, finishing with basil leaves. Spoon 1 tablespoon of the vinaigrette over each tower and another tablespoon around each tower. Sprinkle a pinch of sea salt on each salad and serve at room temperature.

Serves 4 to 6 as a first course

ꞏ Making Mozzarella ꞏ

In Italy, fresh mozzarella is considered past its prime if more than twenty-four hours old. This high-moisture cheese is made with either water buffalo or cow's milk, or a mixture of the two. In a fairly simple two-step process, citric acid or rennet is added to the milk to form curds. The curds are cut into small pieces and mixed with hot water and then stretched by hand or machine to form into smooth, elastic ropes or rolled into balls of varying sizes. The cheese is then placed in a cold brine of water and salt to preserve it until use. Fresh mozzarella can be found in most markets in the dairy or cheese section.

Shaved Zucchini and Pecorino Cheese Salad

Marché aux Fleurs, Ross

*Marché aux Fleurs shows off summer zucchini with this unique
yet simple salad served with shaved cheese and Spanish almonds. Another dry sheep's
milk cheese such as Manchego may be used.*

◦⍟ Marché aux Fleurs ⍟◦

Named after a famed flower market in Nice,
the Ross restaurant bases its cuisine on
locally farmed seasonal produce, wild seafood, and free-range meats as the stars of
the menu. The impressive wine list features
small family-run wineries—perfect to pair
with organic entrées like braised short ribs
with celery root puree and roasted carrots,
or English pea ravioli with mint ricotta and
brown butter.

Vinaigrette
2 tablespoons freshly squeezed
  lemon juice
1 teaspoon Dijon mustard
⅓ cup extra-virgin olive oil
¼ teaspoon kosher salt
⅛ teaspoon freshly ground
  pepper

3 zucchini or yellow squash
1 bunch baby arugula
½ cup shaved pecorino cheese
¼ cup Marcona almonds,
  chopped

For the vinaigrette: Whisk the lemon juice and mustard
together in a small bowl. Gradually whisk in the olive oil
and the salt and pepper. Set aside.

Using a mandoline or vegetable peeler, cut the zucchini
into thin lengthwise strips. Place in a large bowl with the
arugula and pecorino. Lightly toss the vegetables with the
dressing and place in a serving bowl or individual plates.
Garnish with the almonds and serve.

Serves 4 as a first course

Grilled Pork Tenderloin and Nectarines with Bacon Vinaigrette

Picco, Larkspur

*Fresh stone fruit is an ideal complement to pork. Picco serves
this sweet and savory recipe with local nectarines in summer, and persimmons in fall.
Plums or apricots are also delicious when grilled.*

Bacon Vinaigrette

3 ounces diced pancetta
2 tablespoons minced shallots
½ teaspoon brown sugar
¼ cup red wine vinegar
½ cup extra-virgin olive oil
½ teaspoon salt
¼ teaspoon freshly ground
  pepper

1½-pound pork tenderloin
2 firm nectarines, quartered
2 tablespoons canola oil
Salt and freshly ground pepper
1 head frisée lettuce or small
  bunch arugula

For the vinaigrette: Heat a small sauté pan over medium heat and cook the pancetta for 3 minutes, until golden. Add the shallots and sauté for 2 minutes. Remove the pan from the heat and stir in the sugar and vinegar. Gradually whisk in the olive oil, then whisk in the salt and pepper. Set aside until ready to serve.

Preheat a hot fire in a charcoal grill or preheat a gas grill to high. Season the pork tenderloin and nectarines generously with 2 tablespoons of oil, salt, and pepper. Oil the grill grids and place the pork and nectarines on the grill and sear for about 5 minutes, or until both are browned on all sides. Turn off the heat or move the tenderloin and fruit to the cool edges of the grill. Cover the grill for 10 minutes.

Reheat the vinaigrette over low heat. Lightly dress the frisée in a bowl and mound on a platter or 4 warmed plates. Cut the pork tenderloin into ½-inch-thick slices and place with the nectarines alongside the frisée. Drizzle with the remaining vinaigrette. Serve warm.

Serves 4 as a main course

⤳ Picco ⤳

Since opening in 2005, Picco has attracted food enthusiasts from around the Bay Area to its Larkspur dining room. Built around the shared small-plate concept, revolving menu selections are guided by local seasonable ingredients, though year-round regulars can count on certain menu items like avocado bruschetta, three grass-fed mini burgers, and the ever-popular risotto.

Chicken Fra Diavolo with Fennel and Dandelion Salad

Incanto, San Francisco

A favorite dish at Incanto is this recipe for marinated and grilled chicken. The spice rub has a wonderful sweet, smoky flavor that would also complement most meats and fish.

◦ **Conventional vs.** ◦
Organic Chickens

Conventional chickens are fed conventional grains. Most of these grains have been treated with pesticides, herbicides, and fertilizers, resulting in chickens that have toxins stored in their fat. Because conventional chickens are often raised in confined quarters with poor-quality food and a lack of exercise, sickness is common. Consequently, antibiotics are used in an attempt to keep the birds healthy. Certified organic chickens have been fed organic grain and are not medicated. This eliminates the risk of humans consuming toxins, antibiotics, or hormones. However, "certified organic" does not mean that the animal was allowed to run free. Therefore, "organic free-range" chickens are the healthiest choice, since these chickens were not caged and were fed organic food.

1 (4-pound) chicken

Marinade
6 cloves garlic
1 red Fresno chili, seeded
1 serrano chili, seeded
1 teaspoon sweet pimentón (Spanish smoked paprika)
1 teaspoon kosher salt
½ teaspoon freshly ground black pepper
½ teaspoon red pepper flakes
1 tablespoon fresh thyme leaves
1 bay leaf
Zest and juice of 1 orange
½ cup olive oil

Vinaigrette
Juice of 1 lemon
¼ cup extra-virgin olive oil, plus more for drizzling
¼ teaspoon salt
⅛ teaspoon freshly ground pepper

1 fennel bulb, trimmed and shaved
8 ounces dandelion greens or arugula leaves

Use a pair of kitchen shears to remove the backbone of the chicken by cutting along both sides of the bone. Reserve the backbone for another use. Flatten the chicken with the heel of your hand and place in a large, resealable plastic bag.

For the marinade: Combine all the ingredients in a food processor and puree to a smooth paste. Pour the marinade into the bag with the chicken, seal, and mix well. Refrigerate for at least 4 hours, or preferably overnight.

Remove the chicken from the refrigerator 30 minutes before cooking. Prepare a hot fire in a charcoal grill, or preheat a gas grill to high; also preheat an oven to 350°F. Oil the grill grids and sear the chicken, bone side down, for 7 to 10 minutes, until crisp and brown. Flip the chicken over and grill on the other side until brown, 7 to 10 minutes. Transfer the chicken to a baking sheet

(continued on next page)

Chicken Fra Diavolo with Fennel and Dandelion Salad

(continued)

and roast in the oven for 25 minutes or until an instant-read thermometer inserted in the thigh registers 165°F. Set the chicken aside and let rest for 10 minutes.

For the vinaigrette: Whisk the lemon juice, ¼ cup olive oil, salt, and pepper together in a small bowl until well combined. Put the fennel and dandelion greens in a large bowl and toss well with the vinaigrette.

Using a large chef's knife, cut the chicken into 4 serving pieces. Divide the salad among 4 plates and top each serving with a piece of chicken. Drizzle with extra-virgin olive oil and serve immediately.

Serves 4 to 6 as a main course

Harvesting dandelion greens at Marin Roots Farm near Petaluma.

Pan-Roasted Salmon with Tomatoes and Corn

Drake's Beach Café, Inverness

Drake's Beach Café prepares perfectly cooked salmon with a mélange of local summer vegetables. The salmon should be served slightly undercooked to ensure a moist fillet.

Tomatoes and Corn

1 tablespoon canola oil

1 tablespoon unsalted butter

2 tablespoons minced shallots

2 cups corn kernels (about 3 ears)

1½ cups multicolored cherry
  tomatoes, halved

1 tablespoon minced fresh basil

1 tablespoon minced fresh chives,
  plus more for garnish

1 teaspoon freshly squeezed
  lemon juice

¼ teaspoon kosher salt

⅛ teaspoon freshly ground
  pepper

4 (6-ounce) king salmon fillets,
  pin bones removed

¼ teaspoon kosher salt

⅛ teaspoon freshly ground
  pepper

2 tablespoons canola oil

1 teaspoon white truffle oil

For the tomatoes and corn: Heat a large sauté pan over high heat. Add the oil and butter and sauté the shallots for 2 minutes, until they begin to soften. Add the corn and tomatoes and sauté for 2 to 3 minutes, until the tomatoes just release their juices. Remove from the heat and stir in the fresh herbs, lemon juice, salt, and pepper to taste.

Season the salmon fillets with salt and pepper. Heat a large nonstick sauté pan over high heat. Add the oil to the pan and sear the fillets, skin side down, for 3 to 4 minutes, until golden brown and crisp. Repeat on the other side.

To serve, put 2 heaping tablespoons of the vegetables in the center of each of 4 warmed plates. Top each with a piece of salmon, skin side up. Drizzle ¼ teaspoon of truffle oil around each plate and garnish with the chives. Serve immediately.

Serves 4 as a main course

⤜ Heirloom Tomatoes ⤚

Heirloom tomatoes are old-fashioned, or "antique," varieties of the fruit. Available in many different varieties with diverse characteristics, heirloom tomatoes are prized for their spectrum of colors and distinctive flavors. Sizes range from bite-sized tomatoes to individual fruits weighing two pounds. When selecting heirlooms in the market, choose a lighter color tomato for a less acidic and sweeter fruit, and a more deeply colored one for a more assertive taste.

Seared Ahi Tuna with Asian Slaw

Buckeye Roadhouse, Mill Valley

One of Buckeye Roadhouse's hit appetizers, this Asian-inspired seared tuna is a terrific combination of textures and flavors. The wonton strips may be fried ahead of time and kept crisp for several days in a sealed container.

❧ Buckeye Roadhouse ❧

Feeding locals and tourists since the 1930s, the Buckeye serves gourmet versions of traditional American roadhouse fare, like New York steak, baby back ribs, and garlic fries. The restaurant, which is bustling every night of the week, has a hunting lodge atmosphere, with stuffed animal trophies, a vaulted ceiling, and a massive stone fireplace. Whether you're seated at the bar, in the restaurant, or, weather permitting, on the outdoor patio, the Buckeye should not be missed.

2 cups shredded napa cabbage
1 cup shredded red cabbage
1 cup green beans, trimmed and thinly sliced lengthwise
½ cup thinly sliced red bell pepper
¼ cup chopped pickled ginger
¼ cup coarsely chopped fresh cilantro

Wonton Strips
½ cup canola oil
6 square wonton sheets, cut into ⅛-inch-wide strips

Dressing
2 tablespoons peeled, chopped ginger
2 tablespoons chopped green onion (including green parts)
2 cloves garlic
1 tablespoon chopped fresh cilantro
⅓ cup hoisin sauce
3 tablespoons water
3 tablespoons rice vinegar
2 tablespoons soy sauce

1 tablespoon ketchup
1 tablespoon toasted sesame oil
2 dashes Tabasco sauce
½ teaspoon sugar

1 pound sashimi-grade ahi tuna
1 tablespoon canola oil
½ teaspoon kosher salt
¼ teaspoon freshly ground pepper
¼ cup sesame seeds

Combine the cabbages, green beans, red bell pepper, pickled ginger, and cilantro in a large bowl. Cover and refrigerate.

Heat the canola oil to 325°F in a small saucepan. Carefully fry the wonton strips for 3 to 4 seconds, until golden brown. Using a slotted spoon, transfer the strips to a paper towel to drain. Set aside.

For the dressing: Blend the ginger, green onion, garlic, and cilantro together in a blender or food processor. Add all the remaining dressing ingredients and process until smooth.

(continued on next page)

Seared Ahi Tuna with Asian Slaw
(continued)

Coat the tuna with the oil and season with the salt and pepper. Scatter the sesame seeds on a plate and press the tuna into the seeds on both sides, gently shaking off the excess. Heat a large grill or sauté pan over high heat and sear the tuna for 3 minutes on each side. Be careful not to burn the sesame seeds. Remove the fish from the pan and let rest for several minutes before slicing. The tuna will be medium-rare.

To serve, toss the vegetables with half of the dressing and mix well. Add half of the wonton strips and gently combine. Mound the slaw onto a platter or divide among 4 plates. Cut the tuna against the grain into 1-inch-thick slices. Place on top of the salad, drizzle the remaining dressing on top, and garnish with the remaining wonton strips.

Serves 4 as a first course

Colorful green and purple cabbages at the Marin Farmers' Market and in the field at Gospel Flat Farm in Bolinas.

Wok-Tossed Blue Lake Beans

Harmony Restaurant, Mill Valley

The chefs at Harmony insist that only the freshest ingredients are served at this Cantonese-inspired restaurant. This is a simple and healthy way of serving one of summer's best vegetables. The technique of blanching followed by stir-frying keeps the beans crisp and vibrant.

¼ cup chicken or vegetable stock
1 teaspoon cornstarch
Pinch of ground white pepper
1 pound green, wax, or Romano beans, trimmed
2 tablespoons canola oil
2 cloves garlic, thinly sliced
1 cup cherry tomatoes, halved

Combine the chicken stock, cornstarch, and white pepper in a small bowl. Stir to blend and place the bowl next to the stove.

In a large pot of salted boiling water, blanch the beans for 3 minutes, until crisp-tender. Drain and plunge into cold water to cool. Drain again and pat the beans dry.

Heat a wok or a large sauté pan over high heat until almost smoking. Add the oil and stir-fry the garlic for several seconds, being careful not to burn it. Add the green beans and tomatoes and stir-fry for 2 minutes, until heated through. Stir the cornstarch mixture again, then stir it into the wok and toss the beans and tomatoes for about 1 minute, or until the sauce thickens. Serve immediately.

Serves 4 to 6 as a side dish

❧ Harmony Restaurant ❧

Dim sum meets local farmers at this popular Chinese food haunt in Mill Valley. The décor is a step above average, and so is the food. Fresh dim sum offerings are served daily, along with a menu of standbys like chow fun, broccoli and beef, and pork buns as well as creative seasonal dishes, all made from organic local foods. Takeout? Of course!

Gypsy Peppers Stuffed with Fromage Blanc

Greens Restaurant, San Francisco

These yellow, pointed peppers (also called bullhorn peppers) are available at local farmers' markets in the late summer and early fall. With their sweet, thick flesh, they are easy to peel and are great for stuffing. Pimientos are another great variety for this recipe.

4 gypsy peppers
2 tablespoons olive oil
½ teaspoon kosher salt, plus
   more for sprinkling
¼ teaspoon freshly ground
   pepper, plus more for sprinkling

Filling

1½ cups fromage blanc, ricotta,
   or fresh goat cheese
1 large egg
1 tablespoon minced fresh
   flat-leaf parsley
1 tablespoon minced fresh
   tarragon
1 tablespoon minced fresh chives
½ teaspoon kosher salt
⅛ teaspoon freshly ground
   pepper

Preheat an oven to 400°F. Rub the peppers with olive oil, the ½ teaspoon salt, and the ¼ teaspoon pepper. Place the peppers on a baking sheet and roast for 15 to 20 minutes, until the skin is blistered and the flesh is soft. Remove from the oven and let cool to the touch. Peel the peppers, being careful to remove the skin around the stems, leaving the stems in place. Make a lengthwise slit into each pepper and remove the seeds Sprinkle the peppers with more salt and pepper.

Decrease the oven temperature to 375°F. Oil a baking sheet.

For the filling: Combine all the ingredients in a medium bowl and mix well. Gently spoon ¼ cup of the filling into each pepper. Place the peppers, seam side down, on the prepared pan. Bake for 25 to 30 minutes, until the peppers are puffed and the filling is set. Serve warm.

Serves 4 as a first course

✒ Green Gulch Farm ✑

Green Gulch Farm, also known as Green Dragon Temple, is located in Muir Beach just north of the Golden Gate Bridge. Part of the San Francisco Zen Center, it is a Zen monastery, a conference site, and a working farm supplying fresh, organic produce for Greens Restaurant in San Francisco and selling its produce at local farmers' markets.

Fresh Fruit Scones

Rustic Bakery, Larkspur

A favorite at the Rustic Bakery, these moist fruit-filled scones can be served for breakfast or as a shortcake with crème fraîche for dessert. The recipe adapts to the seasons: Try juicy figs in fall and creamy pears in winter.

2 ¼ cups all-purpose flour

⅓ cup sugar

1 tablespoon baking powder

½ teaspoon salt

¼ teaspoon baking soda

¾ cup (1 ½ sticks) cold unsalted butter, cut into small pieces

¾ cup buttermilk

1 ½ cups ½-inch-diced fresh fruit (such as peaches, strawberries, blueberries, or blackberries)

1 large egg, beaten

2 tablespoons heavy cream

2 tablespoons turbinado sugar

Combine the flour, sugar, baking powder, salt, and baking soda in a large bowl and stir with a whisk to blend. Add the butter and cut it into the flour mixture with a pastry cutter to the size of peas. Gradually add the buttermilk to the dough, mixing with your hands until the dough just comes together. Gently mix in the fruit with your hands. If the fruit is juicy, less buttermilk can be used. Do not overmix, or the scones will be tough.

Turn the dough out onto a lightly floured work surface. Divide the dough in half and form each piece into a disk 2 inches thick. Use a knife to cut each disk into 6 even triangles. Line a baking sheet with parchment paper. Place the scones 2 inches apart on the prepared pan and refrigerate for 30 minutes.

Preheat the oven to 375°F. Using a fork or small whisk, beat the egg and cream together in a small bowl. Using a pastry brush, coat the top of each scone with the egg mixture. Sprinkle with the turbinado sugar and bake for 20 to 25 minutes, until a light golden brown. Remove from the oven and transfer the scones to wire racks. Serve warm or at room temperature.

Makes 12 scones

❧ Freezing Berries ❧

The best way to extend the berry season is to freeze surplus berries the day they are picked or purchased. Pick out any stems, dirt, or mold. Wash the berries and gently pat dry with a paper towel. Place the berries in a single layer on a baking sheet lined with parchment paper and freeze for at least 1 hour. Place the frozen berries in a resealable plastic bag, remove any air, and freeze for up to 6 months. The berries do not need to be thawed before using.

fall

A harvest of pumpkins glows in the autumn sun at
Star Route Farms along the shores of Bolinas Lagoon.

*We are indeed much more than what we eat, but what we eat
can nevertheless help us to be much more than what we are.*
—Adelle Davis

fall

If you don't like the weather, as Mark Twain reportedly said about New England, just wait a few minutes and it'll change. Had Twain been commenting on Marin County, though, he would have said: "If you don't like the weather here, just go a few miles and it'll be different." Especially in the fall.

West Marin unfolds across an uneven terrain of hills and valleys. As the main growing season wanes, the fortunes of any farmer's particular field depend on which direction it faces, how long the sun warms it, and whether it traps the cool nighttime air.

The first rains of the wet season also arrive off the Pacific, often appearing as squalls that drench one valley but leave another dry. With some fields several hundred feet higher than others—even on the same farm—this can mean that the moisture that nourishes one type of crop for a few more weeks will finish off others in a few more days.

The fall harvest brings forth the heartier vegetables: winter squashes like acorn, butternut, and the colorful Carnival and Delicata; turnips and red and golden beets; and the final fingerling potatoes dug fresh from the soil (before they're bagged in burlap for winter storage).

Heirloom apples, ripened on decades-old trees in West Marin, also signal the end of summer, finding a place in the market alongside golden pears whose days are passing just in time to make room for persimmons and pomegranates. Right up until the rains saturate the ground, leafy row crops remain in abundance: spinach, kale, chard, and chives. But with each passing week in the market, it is more common to hear a seller say to a disappointed buyer, "Sorry, they're done for the season."

As always, though, loss and gain journey together in the natural cycle. On Marin's dairy farms and beef ranches, where the summer grasses are nothing more than a ruminant's memory, the fall rain elicits immediate growth: a peach fuzz of delicate, wispy green shoots that hold the promise of spring once the coming winter is done.

Crab Cakes with Watercress and Blood Oranges

Drake's Beach Café, Inverness

At Drake's Beach Café, the best crab cakes are made from the Dungeness crab cooked the day they are caught. Watercress and blood oranges add color and a refreshing counterpoint to the fresh seafood. Grapefruit and arugula are also a good combination for this dish.

Chive Oil

¼ cup minced fresh chives

⅓ cup grapeseed oil

⅛ teaspoon salt

Crab Cakes

1 pound fresh lump Dungeness crabmeat, picked over for shell

½ cup crème fraîche

1 large shallot, minced

Grated zest and juice of 1 lemon

1 large egg, beaten

2 cups panko (Japanese bread crumbs)

¼ cup minced mixed fresh herbs (chives, flat-leaf parsley, and tarragon)

½ teaspoon kosher salt, plus more to taste

⅛ teaspoon ground white pepper, plus more to taste

2 tablespoons unsalted butter

2 blood oranges, peeled and segmented, juice reserved (see page 186)

2 tablespoons extra-virgin olive oil

Salt and freshly ground pepper

1 bunch watercress or arugula, stemmed, or leaves from 1 head frisée lettuce

¾ teaspoon aged balsamic vinegar

For the chive oil: Combine all the chive oil ingredients in a blender and puree until smooth. Set aside and let stand for 30 minutes. Strain the mixture through a fine-meshed sieve. Discard the solids and reserve the oil. The chive oil keeps refrigerated for 4 days.

For the crab cakes: Combine the crabmeat, crème fraîche, shallot, lemon zest and juice, egg, 1 cup of the panko, the herbs, salt, and pepper. Firmly pack the crabmeat mixture into a ¼-cup measuring cup and invert onto a baking sheet, repeating to use all of the mixture, yielding 6 crab cakes. Cover and refrigerate for at least 1 hour or up to 4 hours.

(continued on next page)

◡❧ Dungeness Crab ❧◡

Dungeness crab is found along the Pacific Coast from Alaska to northern California. Weighing from one to three pounds, this flavorful crustacean has plentiful meat. Crab season begins in early November and peaks in January in northern California.

One of the best ways to serve fresh Dungeness crab is steamed and eaten with drawn butter. To steam crab, bring 2 inches of water to a boil in the bottom of a pot fitted with a large steamer insert. Place the live crab upside down in the pot and steam, covered, until the shell turns bright orange, 12 to 15 minutes. Remove from the pot and let cool.

To remove the meat, pull the apron off the underside of the crab and lift off the carapace. Discard the feathery gills and mandibles from the body and rinse the crab under cool water. Grip the crab on either side and break it in half. Remove the legs and claws from the body and crack them at the edge of the joints with a small mallet. Remove the meat from the body sections and serve with the legs and claws.

Crab Cakes with Watercress and Blood Oranges

(continued)

Preheat an oven to 250°F. Line a baking sheet with parchment paper. Place the remaining 1 cup panko on a plate and season with salt and pepper to taste. Melt the butter in a large nonstick sauté pan over medium heat. Dredge the crab cakes in the panko to coat evenly and sear for 5 to 7 minutes on each side, until golden brown. Transfer to the prepared pan and keep warm in the oven while finishing the dish.

Whisk 1 tablespoon of the reserved blood orange juice, the olive oil, salt, and pepper together in a small bowl to make a vinaigrette.

To serve, place a crab cake on each of 6 salad plates. Dress the watercress and orange segments with the vinaigrette and place a small handful alongside each crab cake. Drizzle 1/8 teaspoon of the balsamic vinegar and 1 teaspoon of the chive oil around each serving. Serve immediately.

Serves 6 as a first course

Roasted Red Pepper Bisque

Small Shed Flatbreads, Mill Valley

*Small Shed Flatbreads serves this popular tomato-based soup
all year round. Roasted peppers lend the soup a wonderful smoky flavor.
For extra heat, add more roasted jalapenos and pimentón.*

❧ Roasting Peppers ❧

Roasted peppers impart a delicious smoky flavor to any dish. For a small quantity of peppers, place them directly over a gas flame and turn them with tongs until the skin is evenly charred black on all sides. To broil, place the whole peppers on a broiler pan an inch or two from the heating element until blistered and charred. Use tongs to turn the peppers until charred on all sides. Place the roasted peppers in a plastic bag and seal the bag. Allow the peppers to sweat for 10 minutes, then peel and remove the stems, veins, and seeds if necessary.

2 large red bell peppers
1 jalapeño chili
3 tablespoons canola oil
1 large yellow onion, chopped
3 cloves garlic, minced
1 teaspoon sweet pimentón
  (Spanish smoked paprika)
½ tablespoon kosher salt
¼ teaspoon freshly ground
  pepper
1½ pounds tomatoes, peeled,
  seeded, and chopped
6 cups vegetable or chicken stock
2 tablespoons minced fresh basil,
  plus 4 fresh basil leaves, cut
  into fine shreds
1 tablespoon minced fresh
  flat-leaf parsley
¼ cup crème fraîche

Roast the red peppers and jalapeño according to the instructions at left. Place the roasted peppers in a large bowl and cover with plastic wrap. Let sweat for 10 minutes.

Heat a large stockpot over high heat. Add the oil and sauté the onion for 3 to 4 minutes, until translucent. Add the garlic, pimentón, salt, and pepper and sauté for 5 minutes. Decrease the heat to medium, stir in the tomatoes, and simmer for 15 minutes. Meanwhile, carefully peel the charred skins from the warm peppers and remove the seeds and stems. Chop the peppers and add to the tomatoes. Stir in the stock, the 2 tablespoons basil, and the parsley. Simmer for 30 minutes.

Puree the soup in batches in a blender or food processor until smooth. Be careful not to overfill the blender. Return the soup to a clean pot and reheat. Adjust the seasoning.

To serve, spoon the soup into warmed bowls. Garnish each with a dollop of crème fraîche and a sprinkling of shredded basil. Serve hot.

Serves 4 to 6 as a first course

Grilled Fig and Mâche Salad

Olema Inn & Restaurant, Olema

The Olema Inn & Restaurant serves this warm salad with local figs from Blackberry Farm in Bolinas and Red Hawk Cheese from Cowgirl Creamery. This dish is also delicious with grilled seasonal stone fruits and other washed-rind cheeses.

Vinaigrette

⅓ cup sherry vinegar

1 cinnamon stick

2 bay leaves

6 allspice berries

1 star anise pod

1 tablespoon brown sugar

¼ cup hazelnut oil

¼ cup olive oil

Salt and freshly ground pepper

2 teaspoons olive oil

8 figs, stemmed and halved

Salt and freshly ground pepper

4 ounces Cowgirl Creamery Red Hawk Cheese (Port Salut or Pont L'Eveque may be substituted)

8 ounces mâche

⅛ cup red onion, thinly sliced

1 small fennel bulb, trimmed, cored, and thinly sliced

¼ cup hazelnuts, toasted, skinned, and chopped (see page 186)

For the vinaigrette: Combine the vinegar and spices in a small stainless-steel pan and simmer over low heat until steam rises. Remove from the heat, stir in the brown sugar, and let steep for 30 minutes. Strain into a small bowl and discard the spices. Gradually whisk in the hazelnut and olive oils. Season with salt and pepper to taste. Set aside.

Prepare a medium fire in a charcoal grill, preheat a gas grill to 375°F, or heat a grill pan over medium heat. Rub 1 teaspoon of oil on the grill or pan. Season the figs with 1 teaspoon of oil, salt, and pepper. Grill the figs, skin side down, until the centers of the figs begin to bubble, 3 to 5 minutes. Repeat on the other side. Remove from the heat and keep warm.

Cut the cheese into thin wedges and place 2 wedges on each of 4 salad plates. Place 4 fig halves next to the cheese. Combine the mâche, onion, fennel, and hazelnuts in a large bowl. Lightly dress the salad, tossing to just coat the leaves. Mound in the center of the salad plates. Drizzle the remaining vinaigrette around the salad plate and serve.

Serves 4 as a first course

◡ Olema Inn & Restaurant ◠

This 1876 country inn and restaurant, nestled in West Marin, is a favorite spot for relaxing on the garden patio with a bottle of California wine and items off the chef's organic and sustainable menu. Inside, the 75-seat dining room features a simple interior with paned windows, pine floors, and white tablecloths. Locals says the Tomales Bay Hog Island oysters on the half shell are not to be missed; they're served with any of eight combinations of toppings ranging from classic French Champagne vinegar to spring peas and lavender. For a heartier appetizer, try the charcuterie and cheese plate featuring various artisan cheeses from nearby Cowgirl Creamery.

Orecchiette with Sausage Ragù and Broccoli Rabe

Piatti Ristorante & Bar, Mill Valley

This rich, hearty pasta dish uses freshly made pork and fennel sausages.
Broccoli rabe adds texture and an interesting slight bitterness to the sauce.
If broccoli rabe is unavailable, broccoli florets can be substituted.

✆ Broccoli Rabe ✆

At first glance, broccoli rabe, or rapini, appears like domestic broccoli. On closer look, the stems are longer and thinner, the florets are quite small, and there are more leaves. A relative of spinach, kale, and bok choy, broccoli rabe can be found year-round but is more abundant in the spring and summer. Unlike common broccoli, rapini has a pungent-bitter flavor, which is lessened with steaming or sautéing. A classic Italian favorite, broccoli rabe has gained popularity and has made its way into most produce sections.

2 tablespoons olive oil
1 pound spicy pork-fennel sausages, casings removed
4 ounces pancetta, finely chopped
1 small red onion, chopped
2 cloves garlic, minced
1½ cups dry red wine
3 cups canned tomatoes, coarsely chopped, or 6 fresh tomatoes, chopped
1 cup water
½ tablespoon minced marjoram
¼ teaspoon kosher salt
⅛ teaspoon freshly ground pepper
1 bunch broccoli rabe, coarsely chopped
1 pound orecchiette pasta
½ cup grated pecorino cheese

Heat a large saucepan over medium-high heat, add the oil, and sauté the sausage meat and pancetta for 7 to 10 minutes, until lightly browned. Using a slotted spoon, transfer the meat to a bowl. Pour off all but 1 tablespoon of the oil. Add the onion and sauté over medium heat for 3 minutes, until translucent. Stir in the garlic and return the meat to the pan. Add the wine and cook to reduce the liquid by half. Add the tomatoes, water, marjoram, and salt and pepper. Reduce the heat and simmer for 1 hour.

Cook the broccoli rabe in a large pot of salted boiling water for about 5 minutes. Using tongs, transfer the greens to a bowl and reserve the water for cooking the pasta.

Bring the reserved water to a boil. Add the broccoli rabe to the sausage mixture. Cook the pasta for 8 to 10 minutes, or until al dente, and drain, reserving ¼ cup of the pasta water. Return the pasta and reserved water to the pot, add three-fourths of the sauce to the pasta, and toss.

To serve, divide the pasta among warmed shallow bowls. Spoon the remaining sauce on top and serve with the pecorino cheese at the table.

Serves 4 to 6 as a main course

Blood Orange and Star Anise–Braised Pork

Farmhouse Inn, Forestville

The Farmhouse Inn in nearby Sonoma County prepares this wonderful dish with pork shank. However, pork shoulder is more readily available and is also incredibly tender when braised in this piquant sauce of orange and anise. The kitchen suggests serving sautéed kale as an accompaniment. Start the braised pork 1 day before serving.

2½ pounds boneless pork shoulder

1 tablespoon ground fennel

1 teaspoon kosher salt

½ teaspoon freshly ground pepper

2 tablespoons olive oil

4 ounces pancetta, diced

1 small yellow onion, diced

2 small carrots, peeled and diced

3 stalks celery, diced

2 cloves garlic, minced

3 star anise pods

1 cup dry red wine

4 cups chicken stock

3 blood oranges or 2 navel oranges, peeled and sliced

Preheat an oven to 300°F. Heat a Dutch oven or large, heavy ovenproof sauté pan over medium-high heat. Season the pork with the ground fennel, salt, and pepper. Add the oil to the pan and sear the meat for 15 minutes, until browned on all sides. Transfer the meat to a plate.

In the same pan, sauté the pancetta, onion, carrots, celery, and garlic for about 7 minutes, or until the vegetables are crisp-tender. Stir in the star anise, wine, and stock and bring to a boil. Decrease the heat to a simmer and add the sliced oranges. Return the roast to the pan.

Cover the pan tightly with aluminum foil, then a lid. Braise in the oven for 3 hours, until fork-tender. Remove from the oven and let cool. Cover and refrigerate overnight.

Preheat an oven to 400°F. Remove the roast from the sauce. Spoon off the fat and bring the sauce to a boil over high heat. Strain the sauce through a sieve. Return the roast to the empty pan and pour the sauce over it. Reheat in the oven for 30 minutes, basting occasionally. Remove from the oven. Taste and adjust the seasoning. Cut the meat into slices and serve warm, with the sauce.

Serves 4 to 6 as a main course

ᷓ Blood Oranges ᷓ

Blood oranges have a crimson flesh with a skin that may be tinged with red as well. Cultivated in Sicily since ancient times, the distinctive dark flesh of blood oranges is due to the presence of *anthocyanin,* a pigment common to many red fruits and flowers, but uncommon in citrus fruits. Juicy and sweet, these oranges have slight raspberry and strawberry overtones and are a bit less acidic than regular table oranges. The three main varieties—the Moro, Sanguigno, and Tarocco—are mainly grown in California and Texas and are available from December through March. Select thin-skinned fruit that is firm and heavy for its size.

Plantains Stuffed with Ground Beef

Sol Food, San Rafael

This authentic Puerto Rican eatery in San Rafael serves delicious plantain dishes. Whether roasted or fried, they are an absolute hit. Be sure to select ripe plantains, which are yellow with many black markings.

ꙮ **Choosing Plantains** ꙮ

Plantains are firmer and starchier than regular bananas. As they ripen, plantains become sweeter, and their color changes from green to yellow and then to black. Unlike regular bananas, they are always cooked, usually by baking, steaming, or frying. Plantains in the yellow to black stages are used in sweet dishes, while less-ripe ones are better for savory dishes.

Canola oil for deep-frying, plus 2 tablespoons
4 large, ripe plantains, peeled
½ teaspoon kosher salt
¼ teaspoon freshly ground pepper
8 ounces ground beef
2 cloves garlic, minced
⅓ cup sofrito (see page 175)
½ cup tomato sauce
½ teaspoon dried oregano
½ cup Spanish olives, pitted
1 cup shredded Monterey jack cheese

Line a baking sheet with paper towels. Heat 3 inches of the oil to 325°F in a large, heavy saucepan over high heat. Fry the plantains, in batches if necessary, for 5 to 7 minutes, until lightly golden brown on all sides. Using a slotted spoon, gently transfer them to the paper-lined pan to soak up excess oil; let cool. Using a paring knife, cut a lengthwise pocket, ½ inch deep and ¼ inch wide, in each plantain, leaving ½ inch uncut at each end. Gently remove the center pieces with the seeds from the plantains and discard. Season the plantains with half of the salt and pepper. Set aside.

Preheat an oven to 375°F. Heat a large sauté pan over high heat, add the 2 tablespoons oil, and sauté the ground beef until browned, breaking up the pieces with a spoon. Add the remaining salt and pepper, garlic, and sofrito and sauté for 5 minutes. Stir in the tomato sauce, oregano, and olives. Simmer over low heat for 15 minutes.

Lay the plantains side by side in a baking dish and stuff them with the beef mixture. Top with the shredded cheese, cover with aluminum foil, and bake for 40 minutes. Uncover the plantains and bake for about 10 minutes, or until the cheese browns. Remove from the oven and serve.

Serves 4 to 6 as a main course

Grilled Swordfish Peperonata

MarketBar, San Francisco

*In this recipe, grilled fish is accented with peperonata,
a classic Mediterranean dish of braised peppers and onions. Try it also
with grilled chicken and as a topping for grilled bread.*

4 (8-ounce) swordfish steaks,
1 inch thick

Marinade

2 tablespoons olive oil

1 tablespoon freshly squeezed
lemon juice

1 clove garlic, minced

1 tablespoon minced fresh
oregano

¼ teaspoon kosher salt

⅛ teaspoon freshly ground
pepper

Peperonata

2 tablespoons olive oil

1 small yellow onion, thinly sliced

1 small fennel bulb, trimmed,
cored, and thinly sliced

1 red bell pepper, seeded,
deribbed, and thinly sliced

1 yellow bell pepper, seeded,
deribbed, and thinly sliced

1 clove garlic, minced

2 small tomatoes, seeded and
chopped

1 tablespoon minced fresh marjoram

1 tablespoon minced fresh flat-leaf parsley

½ teaspoon sherry vinegar

½ teaspoon kosher salt

¼ teaspoon freshly ground pepper

One hour before grilling the swordfish, marinate the fish by placing it in a resealable plastic bag. Combine all the ingredients for the marinade in a small bowl and pour over the fish. Turn to coat and set aside while preparing the peperonata. If not using a grill pan, preheat a gas or charcoal grill to medium heat 30 minutes before cooking.

For the peperonata: Heat a large sauté pan over medium-high heat, add the oil, and sauté the onion and fennel for about 10 minutes, or until just tender. Add the bell peppers and garlic and sauté for about 10 minutes, or until the peppers begin to soften. Stir in the tomatoes and cook for about 5 minutes, or until most of the juices evaporate. Add the fresh herbs and vinegar and simmer for another 2 minutes. Add the salt and pepper. Set aside and keep warm.

(continued on next page)

✑ Grilling Fish ✑

Grilling is a quick method of preparing moist, flavorful fish. Firm-fleshed fish such as salmon, bluefish, striped bass, tuna, and swordfish, and small whole fish like red snapper and trout, are best for grilling. Prepare a medium-hot fire in a charcoal grill or preheat a gas grill to medium. Oil the grill grids and place the fish fillets, skin side down, on the grate several inches apart. Grill until ¼ inch of the bottom of the fillet is opaque and has a crust, about 2 minutes. Turn the fillet over with a spatula and grill the other side for 1 minute. Do not flip the fish more than once. Turn off the grill, leave the fillet on the grill, and cover with a lid for another 5 minutes. The fish is done when the flesh easily flakes. Some fish, like salmon, should be removed immediately after grilling both sides so the center is still slightly translucent.

Grilled Swordfish Peperonata

(continued)

Heat a grill pan over high heat, if using. Remove the
swordfish from the marinade and pat the steaks dry.
Oil the grill grids or grill pan and sear the fish for 3 to
4 minutes on each side, until golden brown. Transfer the
steaks to 4 warmed plates and spoon 2 heaping tablespoons of peperonata over each. Serve at once.

Serves 4 as a main course

Butternut Squash Gratin

Greens Restaurant, San Francisco

Chef Annie Somerville's rustic gratin is a delightful side dish for an autumn supper. The crisp topping gives way to a tender buttery squash beneath. Because you can make the gratin ahead of time and reheat it at the last minute, this is a great choice for a holiday meal.

✲ Greens Restaurant ✲

The atmosphere at Greens, one of the nation's premiere vegetarian restaurants, is almost as prized as the food. The converted Fort Mason warehouse was transformed into an airy, art-filled dining room in 1979, with massive walnut doors and floor-to-ceiling windows featuring views of a marina, the Golden Gate Bridge, and the Marin headlands. Diners flock to the restaurant for organic pizzas, pastas, and salads made from ingredients produced by local growers, including the San Francisco Zen Center's Green Gulch Farm in Marin.

Parmesan Bread Crumbs
1 ½ tablespoons unsalted butter
½ cup fresh bread crumbs
⅓ cup grated Parmesan cheese

3 pounds (5 cups) butternut
    squash, peeled and cut into
    ¾-inch cubes
2 cloves garlic, minced
2 tablespoons unsalted butter,
    melted
1 tablespoon all-purpose flour
½ teaspoon salt
⅛ teaspoon freshly ground black
    pepper
½ cup half-and-half

For the Parmesan bread crumbs: Melt the butter in a small sauté pan over medium heat. Stir in the bread crumbs and toast, stirring, for 4 to 5 minutes, until golden brown. Remove from the heat, let cool, and toss in a small bowl with the Parmesan cheese. Set aside.

Preheat an oven to 375°F. Butter a 9-by-13-inch baking dish. Put the squash in a large bowl. Stir in the garlic, butter, flour, salt, and pepper. Spoon the mixture into the prepared dish and pour the half-and-half on top. Cover the pan with aluminum foil and bake for 30 minutes. Remove from the oven and sprinkle with the Parmesan bread crumbs. Return to the oven and bake, uncovered, until golden brown and crisp, 15 to 20 minutes. Remove from the oven and serve.

Serves 4 to 6 as a side dish

Gingersnaps

Table Café, Larkspur

Table Café serves homemade gingersnaps that are crisp, light, and loaded with spicy flavor. Serve these with pumpkin ice cream or by themselves with tea.

2½ cups all-purpose flour

2 teaspoons baking soda

2 teaspoons ground ginger

1 teaspoon ground cinnamon

½ teaspoon ground allspice

½ teaspoon salt

¼ teaspoon ground white pepper

1 cup granulated sugar

½ cup packed dark brown sugar

¾ cup (1½ sticks) unsalted butter at room temperature

1 large egg

⅓ cup dark molasses

Combine the flour, baking soda, ginger, cinnamon, allspice, salt, and pepper in a medium bowl and stir with a whisk to blend. Cream the sugars and butter together in a large bowl with a wooden spoon or an electric mixer for 4 to 5 minutes, until light and fluffy. Beat in the egg and then the molasses. Mix in the dry ingredients until well combined. Cover and refrigerate for 30 minutes.

Preheat an oven to 350°F. Line 2 baking sheets with parchment paper. Spoon teaspoonfuls of batter 2 inches apart onto the prepared pan. The dough will spread. Bake the cookies for 8 to 10 minutes, being careful not to brown them. Remove from the oven and let cool for 10 minutes on the baking sheet, then transfer the cookies to a wire rack to cool completely. Store in an airtight container for up to 1 week.

Makes 4 dozen cookies

⊱ Straus Family Creamery ⊰

The Straus family, headed by Bill and Ellen Straus, has been dairy farming in West Marin for more than six decades. In 1994, the farm became the first certified organic dairy farm west of the Mississippi. Today, the Straus family uses its own organic milk and that of a few other local farmers to supply its organic creamery, which produces European-style yogurt, butter, and cream and milk sold in glass bottles.

Apple-Brandy Crisp

Drake's Beach Café, Inverness

This simple fruit crisp is a staple of Drake's Beach Café. Ripe Bartlett pears also work well in this homey dessert.

✦ Drake's Beach Café ✦

You can't go any farther west in Marin County for a good organic meal than Drake's Beach Café, located in the visitors' center at Drakes Beach in the Point Reyes National Seashore. The café, open Friday through Sunday, serves a mix of hearty fare perfect for a post-beach walk and elegant dishes for a romantic dinner, all made with ingredients from local farms and ranches.

Topping

1 cup all-purpose flour

1½ cups rolled oats

¾ cup packed brown sugar

¼ teaspoon salt

½ teaspoon ground cinnamon

¼ teaspoon ground ginger

⅛ teaspoon ground nutmeg

½ cup (1 stick) cold unsalted butter, cut into pieces

6 Gravenstein or Granny Smith apples, peeled, cored, and cut into ¼-inch-thick slices

Grated zest and juice of 1 lemon

2 tablespoons Calvados or brandy

1 tablespoon granulated sugar

For the topping: Combine the flour, oats, brown sugar, salt, cinnamon, ginger, and nutmeg in a food processor. Add the butter and pulse for 2 to 3 seconds, until crumbly. Cover and refrigerate.

Preheat an oven to 350°F. Butter a 9-by-13-inch baking dish. Combine the apples, lemon zest and juice, Calvados, and sugar in a large bowl. Mix well and transfer to a buttered baking dish. Spoon the topping evenly over the apples and pat gently. Bake for 45 to 50 minutes, until golden brown. Remove from the oven, let cool for 15 minutes, and serve with whipped cream or ice cream.

Serves 4 to 6

winter

Cattle graze in pastures of grass turned green by winter rains as the fog advances over a ranch near Marshall.

You don't have to cook fancy or complicated masterpieces—just good food from fresh ingredients.
—Julia Child

winter

Winter in Marin is cool, with periods of rain interspersed with sometimes weeks of sunshine, conditions that enable some organic farmers to keep growing. The number of weekly farmers' markets in the county shrinks from nine to two. On the stands are the cruciferous vegetables (broccoli, cabbage, and cauliflower); the roots (turnips, beets, parsnips, rutabaga, and carrots); artichokes (which love coolness) and peas; and an assortment of cool-weather greens such as arugula, kale, and some lettuces.

For many organic farmers, though, winter is the season of restoration, of giving back to the soil the nourishment it provided to all those delicious spring, summer, and fall crops. The soil is allowed to rest, enjoying a few fallow weeks to let the microbes do their healing work, or is planted with fast-growing cover crops of bell bean, vetch, or other legumes. These add nitrogen to the soil and, when plowed under in the spring, become a "green manure" that feeds the cycle of sustainability.

With each passing week of winter, especially after the turn of the year, nature replenishes the land. Scrubs like the flowering currant can blossom as early as January. A warm day can draw out buds on fruit trees and cause daffodils to bloom in the garden.

A Marin winter, though, can behave like an unwanted houseguest: Just when it seems he's leaving and the goodbyes are being said (finally!), he settles in for another conversation. Organic farmers know too

well the capriciousness of winter. With
spring on the cusp, the temptation is
to furrow and plant, to get that crop in
the ground, all the sooner to get to
market. But winter, like farming, favors
the patient. All things come, spring
among them.

Carrot Flan with Peppercress and Mustard Vinaigrette

Fork Restaurant, San Anselmo

This sweet carrot flan served at Fork is paired with a mustard vinaigrette to serve as a savory first course. The flan may be prepared the day before and unmolded right before serving.

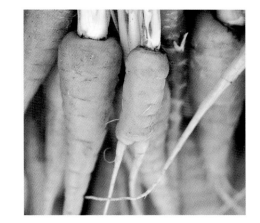

½ cup sugar
¼ cup water
3 cups fresh carrot juice
2 cups chopped carrots
¾ cup heavy cream
1 teaspoon vanilla extract
2 large eggs
2 large egg yolks
1 tablespoon sugar
½ teaspoon salt
⅛ teaspoon freshly ground pepper

Vinaigrette

3 tablespoons Champagne vinegar
1 teaspoon Dijon mustard
1 teaspoon minced fresh tarragon
¼ cup extra-virgin olive oil
¼ teaspoon salt
⅛ teaspoon freshly ground pepper

8 ounces arugula or mixed greens
1 cup baby carrots, blanched for
   5 minutes and diagonally sliced

Combine the sugar and water in a small, heavy saucepan and cook over medium heat, stirring until the sugar is dissolved. Increase the heat to high and cook without stirring until the mixture turns amber. Quickly divide among 6 (4-ounce) ramekins and let cool.

Combine the carrot juice and carrots in a medium saucepan, bring to a boil over medium heat, and decrease the heat to a simmer. Cook for about 10 minutes, or until tender. Pour into a blender and puree until smooth. Strain the pureed carrots through a sieve and return to the saucepan with the cream and vanilla. Heat over medium heat until bubbles form around the edges of the pan.

Preheat an oven to 250°F. Combine the eggs, egg yolks, and sugar in a large bowl and whisk until the mixture is pale yellow and forms a slowly dissolving ribbon when dropped from the whisk onto the surface. Gradually whisk the warm carrot mixture and salt and pepper into the eggs and divide the custard among the ramekins. Place the ramekins in a baking pan and add water to the baking pan to come three-fourths of the way up the sides of the ramekins. Cover the pan with

(continued on next page)

꧁ Carrot Varieties ꧂

This delicious and versatile root vegetable can be eaten raw, made into juice, and cooked in almost any manner imaginable. Other than the standard orange carrots found in all markets, we are seeing more unique varieties that range from white to red to purple. These rainbow varieties of carrots are very flavorful, especially if picked young. Because of the vegetable's inherent sweetness, it historically has been used for desserts as well as savory dishes. Rich in carotene, vitamin A, and fiber, the carrot's healthful qualities make this humble vegetable a dietary star.

Carrot Flan with Peppercress and Mustard Vinaigrette
(continued)

aluminum foil and bake for about 1 1/2 hours, or until firm. Remove from the oven and water and let cool. Refrigerate for at least 4 hours or as long as overnight.

For the vinaigrette: Whisk the vinegar, mustard, and tarragon together in a small bowl until well combined. Gradually whisk in the olive oil, then the salt and pepper.

To serve, run a knife around the edge of each ramekin and invert a flan onto each plate. Dress the arugula and carrots with the vinaigrette and serve alongside the flan.

Serves 6 as a first course

Organic carrots in an array of sizes and colors at the Marin Farmers' Market.

Roasted Butternut Squash Soup

Rustic Bakery, Larkspur

This irresistible soup is served in the fall at the Rustic Bakery. Kabocha and acorn squash are great substitutes for butternut. Leave out the cream for a lighter consistency.

⚜ Roasting Butternut ⚜ Squash

Roasting brings out the best in winter squash. Butternut squash is interchangeable with all hard squashes, such as kabocha, pumpkin, acorn, and Delicata. To roast, preheat an oven to 400°F and line a baking sheet with parchment paper. Carefully cut a 2- to 3-pound butternut squash in half lengthwise and scoop out the seeds. Rub 2 tablespoons of olive oil or melted butter on the cut side of the squash and season with 1/2 teaspoon kosher salt. Place the squash, cut side down, on the prepared pan and roast until fork-tender, 45 to 50 minutes. Remove from the oven and let cool to the touch, then spoon the flesh from the skin and use as the foundation for a soup or side dish.

1 tablespoon olive oil
1 large butternut squash (about 3 pounds), halved and seeded
3/4 teaspoon salt
1/4 teaspoon freshly ground pepper
6 cloves garlic
4 thyme sprigs
3 tablespoons unsalted butter
1 large yellow onion, chopped
3 shallots, chopped
4 cups chicken or vegetable stock
1/4 cup heavy cream

Croutons
1 tablespoon unsalted butter
1 cup 1/2-inch-diced white bread

1 tablespoon crème fraîche
1 tablespoon minced fresh chives

Preheat an oven to 375°F. Line a baking sheet with parchment paper. Rub the olive oil over the cut side of the squash and season with 1/4 teaspoon of the salt and 1/8 teaspoon of the pepper. Place the squash, cut side down, on the prepared pan. Tuck the garlic cloves and thyme sprigs under the cavity of the squash. Roast the squash for 50 to 60 minutes, until soft and caramelized. Remove from the oven and let cool. Reserve the garlic cloves and discard the thyme. Scoop the butternut squash flesh from the skin, coarsely chop, and set aside.

Melt the butter in a Dutch oven or soup pot over medium-high heat. Sauté the onion and shallots for 7 to 10 minutes, until they begin to brown. Add the roasted butternut squash, the reserved garlic cloves, and the remaining 1/2 teaspoon salt and 1/8 teaspoon pepper and sauté for 5 to 7 minutes, until the squash begins to caramelize and stick to the bottom of the pan. Pour in the chicken stock, bring to a boil, then decrease the heat to a simmer and cook for 15 minutes. Puree the soup until smooth with a hand-held blender or in a food processor. Return to the pan if necessary and stir in the cream. Taste and adjust the seasoning.

(continued on next page)

Roasted Butternut Squash Soup

(continued)

For the croutons: Melt the butter in a small sauté pan over medium heat. Stir in the cubes of bread and toast, stirring, for 5 to 7 minutes, until golden brown.

To serve, ladle the hot soup into warmed shallow bowls, dollop each with ½ teaspoon of crème fraîche, and sprinkle with the croutons and chives.

Serves 6 as a first course

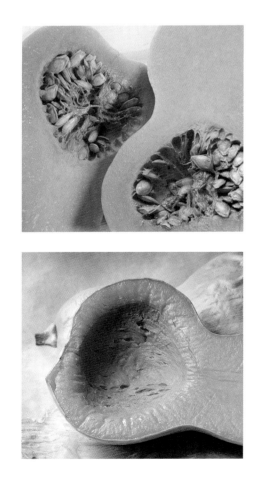

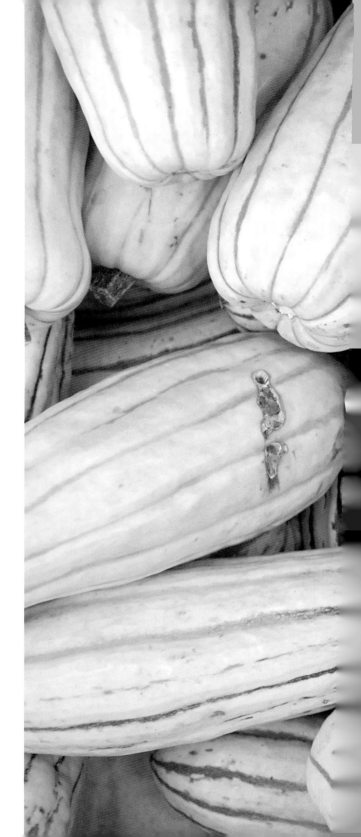

Iceberg Wedges with Blue Cheese Dressing

Small Shed Flatbreads, Mill Valley

Iceberg lettuce is having a comeback! Wedges of organic iceberg make distinctive salads when topped with a creamy, flavorful dressing of crème fraîche and blue cheese. This is a simple and attractive way of serving a tasty lettuce that has fallen by the wayside.

4 ounces pancetta, diced

½ cup crème fraîche

2 tablespoons red wine vinegar

1 tablespoon freshly squeezed
    Meyer lemon juice

½ teaspoon Worcestershire sauce

Pinch of cayenne pepper

½ cup crumbled Point Reyes blue
    cheese

Salt and freshly ground pepper

1 small head iceberg lettuce,
    cored

1 tablespoon minced fresh
    flat-leaf parsley

Cook the pancetta in a small sauté pan over medium heat until crisp and golden brown, about 5 to 10 minutes. Using a slotted spoon, transfer the pancetta to paper towels to drain.

Whisk the crème fraîche, vinegar, lemon juice, Worcestershire sauce, and cayenne pepper together in a large bowl. Whisk in the blue cheese and season with salt and pepper to taste. Cover and refrigerate.

Peel off and discard the outer layer of leaves from the lettuce. Cut the head into quarters and place the wedges, cut side down, on 4 salad plates. Spoon the blue cheese dressing across each wedge and garnish with the pancetta and parsley.

Serves 4 as a first course

❧ Small Shed Flatbreads ❧

Nestled on a quiet side street in downtown Mill Valley, Small Shed Flatbreads has been a local favorite since opening in 2004. Big windows, built-in wooden benches, and large wooden tables add to the casual experience. A wood-burning brick oven positioned just behind the bar is in constant use, creating specialty flat breads made with custom-milled flour and topped with seasonal delicacies. The restaurant's close relationship with neighboring farmers and ranchers is evident in the menu.

Cavolo Nero (Tuscan Braised Kale)

Piatti Ristorante & Bar, Mill Valley

This classic Italian vegetable dish is an excellent accompaniment to braised meats.
Piatti serves this with stracotto, an Italian-style pot roast.

◡ Lacinato Kale ◡

Lacinato kale is a dark, long, leafy green with bumpy leaves. From the cabbage family, its closest relatives are spinach, Swiss chard, and beet and mustard greens. Rich in minerals and vitamins, kale has a slightly bitter flavor that lessens with cooking. Stems and ribs can be tough, so slice or tear the leaves off before washing well in cold water. Kale is delicious boiled, steamed, or braised until tender. Some of the special varieties of kale are collards, Russian kale, and Lacinato (also called dinosaur or Tuscan kale).

¼ cup extra-virgin olive oil
1 yellow onion, thinly sliced
¾ cup water
3 cloves garlic, thinly sliced
½ tablespoon chopped fresh rosemary
¼ teaspoon red pepper flakes
5 cups Lacinato kale (or other kale), stemmed and coarsely chopped
¼ teaspoon kosher salt

Heat the oil in a large sauté pan over medium heat, add the onion, and sauté until just soft, about 5 minutes. Add ¼ cup of the water, cover, and cook the onions until very tender, 7 to 10 minutes. Stir in the garlic, rosemary, and pepper flakes and sauté for 5 minutes. Add the kale and the remaining ½ cup water, cover, and simmer over low heat until the kale is very tender, 30 to 40 minutes. Add more water to the pan if the kale is dry.

Uncover the pan and increase the heat to high to evaporate any excess liquid. Season the kale with salt. Serve warm.

Serves 4 to 6

Kitchen

Not so long ago, it wasn't uncommon to see a horse tied to a post on Main Street in Old Town Novato. Chic boutiques have sprung up alongside old-time candy shops and saloons, creating a rare balance of old and new. Kitchen blends into the mélange with its bright red double door and outdoor seating. The forty-four-seat dining room is built around a state-of-the-art kitchen, where the staff prepares a West Coast version of American comfort food.

Halibut with Rock Shrimp in a Saffron Nage

Kitchen, Novato

*Kitchen highlights fresh halibut and shrimp with a very light saffron butter sauce.
Sea bass and cod are terrific substitutes for the halibut.*

2 tablespoons unsalted butter

4 small leeks (white part only), cut into ¼-inch rings

1 cup water

½ teaspoon salt

Saffron Nage

1 cup dry white wine

8 tablespoons (1 stick) unsalted butter

⅛ teaspoon powdered saffron

¼ teaspoon salt

⅛ teaspoon freshly ground pepper

4 (6-ounce) halibut fillets

¼ teaspoon kosher salt, plus ⅛ teaspoon and a pinch

¼ teaspoon freshly ground pepper, plus a pinch

3 tablespoons canola oil

1 pound spinach, trimmed and washed

2 tablespoons unsalted butter

8 ounces rock shrimp, shelled

1 tablespoon minced fresh flat-leaf parsley

Melt the butter in a medium sauté pan over medium-high heat. Sauté the leeks for 2 minutes, until translucent. Add the water and salt to the leeks and bring to a boil. Decrease the heat to a simmer and braise the leeks for about 30 minutes, or until very tender and most of the liquid evaporates.

For the saffron nage: Bring the wine to a boil in a small saucepan over medium heat. Cook to reduce the wine by half, then remove from the heat. Pour the wine into a blender. With the machine running on the lowest setting, gradually add the butter, 1 tablespoon at a time, until the nage is emulsified. Pour into a bowl and stir in the saffron, salt, and pepper. Keep warm over tepid water.

Preheat an oven to 400°F. Season the halibut fillets with the ¼ teaspoon salt and ⅛ teaspoon of the pepper. Heat a large ovenproof nonstick sauté pan over high heat until almost smoking, then add 2 tablespoons of the oil and sear the fillets for 2 to 3 minutes, until crisp and brown; repeat on the second side. Immediately transfer the pan of fish to the oven and roast for 5 minutes; remove from the oven and keep warm.

(continued on next page)

Halibut with Rock Shrimp in a Saffron Nage

(continued)

While the halibut is in the oven, heat a large sauté pan over high heat, add the remaining 1 tablespoon oil, and sauté the spinach with the 1/8 teaspoon salt and the remaining 1/8 teaspoon pepper until wilted. Remove from the heat and drain in a sieve, pressing on the spinach with the back of a spoon to remove excess moisture. Set aside.

Reheat the same pan over high heat until very hot. Add the butter and rock shrimp. Season with a pinch of salt and pepper and sauté for 2 minutes, until evenly pink on both sides.

To serve, make a ring of leeks on each of 4 warmed plates. Mound the spinach in the center and place the halibut fillets on top of the spinach. Divide the shrimp on top and pour the warm saffron nage around each plate. Garnish with parsley and serve immediately.

Serves 4 as a main course

Tunisian Vegetable Tagine

Insalata's, San Anselmo

Traditional Middle Eastern tagines are prepared in conical-shaped earthenware pots, also called tagines, which cook the contents in their own juices. A Dutch oven or heavy sauté pan is a good substitute. The spice mixture for this Tunisian vegetable stew complements most root and green vegetables.

Spice Mixture

1 teaspoon ground turmeric

1 pinch saffron threads

1 star anise pod

½ teaspoon ground ginger

1 teaspoon ground coriander

1 teaspoon ground cumin

½ teaspoon ground cinnamon

1 teaspoon grated orange zest

⅛ teaspoon freshly ground
pepper

½ teaspoon kosher salt

7 tablespoons extra-virgin olive oil

1 yellow onion, thinly sliced

1 carrot, peeled and cut into
1-inch pieces

1 sweet potato, peeled and cut
into 1-inch pieces

1 parsnip, peeled and cut into
1-inch pieces

1 fennel bulb, trimmed and cut
into ⅛-inch pieces

1 red bell pepper, seeded,
deribbed, and cut into 1-inch
pieces

1 yellow bell pepper, seeded,
deribbed, and cut into 1-inch
pieces

2 zucchini, cut into 1½-inch
pieces

1 cup water

1 (14½-ounce) can peeled and
chopped tomatoes, with juices

1 cup canned chickpeas, drained

½ cup dried currants

Couscous

3 cups vegetable stock

¾ teaspoon salt

1½ cups couscous

2 tablespoons olive oil

½ cup shelled pistachios

1 tablespoon chopped fresh
cilantro for garnish

Combine all the ingredients for the spice mixture in a small bowl and stir to blend. Heat a large Dutch oven or heavy sauté pan over medium heat. Add 3 tablespoons

(continued on the next page)

When Prince Charles and his wife, Camilla, the Duchess of Cornwall, visited West Marin in 2005 to tour organic farms, Peter Martinelli was one of the local farmers invited to dine with them. Martinelli uses the skills he learned while working at Star Route Farms to work more than twenty acres in Bolinas's fertile Paradise Valley. Fresh Run Farm is filled with old-style produce: thick Romano beans, heirloom apples, and De Cicco broccoli, all of it grown organically, the rows painstakingly hoed by hand. "I don't pick a fight with nature," says Peter. "If it needs chemicals to grow, I don't grow it."

Tunisian Vegetable Tagine
(continued)

of oil and sauté the onion for about 7 minutes, or until soft. Stir in all of the spice mixture and sauté for 2 minutes. Transfer the onion mixture to a bowl.

In the same pan, heat 2 tablespoons of the oil over medium heat and sauté the carrot, sweet potato, and parsnip for 10 to 12 minutes, until crisp-tender. Using a slotted spoon, transfer to the bowl with the onion. Reheat the pan, add 2 tablespoons of oil, and sauté the fennel and peppers for 5 minutes, until crisp-tender. Add the zucchini and cook for 5 more minutes.

Return all the vegetables and onion mixture to the pan. Add the water and the tomatoes and their juices and simmer for 15 minutes. Stir in the chickpeas and currants and simmer for 15 to 20 minutes, until the vegetables are tender. Taste and adjust the seasoning.

Just before serving, make the couscous: Combine the stock and salt in a medium saucepan and bring to a bowl. Whisk in the couscous and olive oil. Turn off the heat and cover the pot with a lid. Let stand for 7 to 10 minutes. Fluff with a fork and fold in the pistachios. Serve warm, with the vegetable tagine. Garnish the tagine with the cilantro.

Serves 6 as a main course

Braised Short Ribs with Candied Meyer Lemon Gremolata

AVA Restaurant, San Anselmo

This sweet-and-savory play on braised short ribs is incredibly good. The candied lemon and fresh herbs are a welcoming accent to the richness of the beef. The gremolata would also be a great accompaniment to veal shanks or oxtails.

2½ pounds beef short ribs, cut crosswise into 3-inch-long pieces

2 tablespoons kosher salt, plus ½ teaspoon

2 tablespoons canola oil

1 large yellow onion, cut into ½-inch dice

2 carrots, peeled and cut into ½-inch dice

3 stalks celery, cut into ½-inch dice

2 tablespoons tomato paste

1½ cups dry white wine

6 cups veal or beef stock

1 fresh or 2 dried bay leaves

5 thyme sprigs

⅛ teaspoon freshly ground pepper

Gremolata

1 Meyer lemon

¼ cup water

¼ cup sugar

2 cloves garlic, minced

½ cup firmly packed fresh flat-leaf parsley leaves, minced

¼ teaspoon kosher salt

⅛ teaspoon freshly ground pepper

The day before serving, put the ribs in a bowl and coat evenly with the 2 tablespoons salt. Cover and refrigerate.

The next day, remove the short ribs from the refrigerator 30 minutes before cooking. To cook, heat a large Dutch oven or ovenproof sauté pan over medium-high heat. Add the oil and sear the meat sides of the salted short ribs until dark brown. Do not sear the bone side, to prevent the meat from falling off the bone during braising. Transfer the ribs to a plate. Drain the fat from the pan and reheat the pan over medium heat. Add the onion, carrots, and celery and sauté for 10 to 15 minutes, until they begin to brown. Stir in the tomato paste and cook for 5 minutes, until the paste turns a dark mahogany color. Add the white wine and stir to scrape up the browned bits from the bottom of the pan. Cook for 5 to 7 minutes, or until the liquid is reduced to about ¼ cup. Add the veal stock, bay leaf, and thyme and bring the liquid to a boil over medium-high heat and cook for 15 to 20 minutes to reduce the liquid by half. Season with ½ teaspoon of salt and ⅛ teaspoon of pepper. Strain into a bowl, pressing with the back of

(continued on next page)

Braised Short Ribs with
Candied Meyer Lemon Gremolata
(continued)

a spoon to push the solids through the sieve. Discard the vegetables and herbs.

Preheat the oven to 275°F. Return the seared short ribs to the pan. Pour the strained liquid over the ribs, cover with aluminum foil or a tight lid, and braise in the oven for 3 to 4 hours, until the meat is fork-tender.

While the meat braises, make the gremolata: Using a vegetable peeler, strip off the lemon zest and cut into fine julienne. Reserve the lemon for another use. Put the zest in a small saucepan and cover with water. Bring to a boil over high heat, then drain the lemon through a sieve. Repeat this process 2 more times to take away any bitterness. Add the ¼ cup water and the sugar to the lemon zest. Reduce the heat to medium and cook for 10 to 15 minutes, until the zest becomes translucent and the liquid is syrupy. Drain into a bowl, reserving the syrup for another use, and spread the zest on a plate to dry for 1 hour, until the zest begins to harden. Combine the garlic, parsley, salt, and pepper in a small bowl. Mince the candied lemon, add to the bowl, and mix well.

Taste and adjust the seasoning for the short ribs. Place 2 to 3 pieces of ribs on each warmed plate and spoon a little of the braising liquid over the ribs. Garnish with a pinch of the gremolata and serve. Pass the extra gremolata at the table.

Serves 4 to 6 as a main course

Arroz con Pollo

Sol Food, San Rafael

A basic seasoning mixture for many Puerto Rican dishes is sofrito, which always includes onion, bell pepper, and garlic. Similar to a Spanish paella, this rice dish is packed with flavor and may also be prepared with a combination of sausages and seafood.

1 (4-pound) chicken, cut into
   8 serving pieces

Marinade

¼ cup olive oil

3 cloves garlic, minced

1 tablespoon salt

½ teaspoon freshly ground
   pepper

1 tablespoon dried oregano

Sofrito

2 cloves garlic

¼ cup yellow onion, coarsely
   chopped

¼ cup green bell pepper, seeded,
   deribbed, and coarsely
   chopped

3 tablespoons chopped fresh
   cilantro leaves

½ tablespoon kosher salt

¼ teaspoon freshly ground
   pepper

2 tablespoons canola oil

1 yellow onion, diced

1 red bell pepper, seeded,
   deribbed, and diced

2 cups tomato sauce

2½ cups water

¼ teaspoon kosher salt

2 cups long-grain rice

1 cup small Spanish olives with
   pimientos

1 red bell pepper, roasted,
   peeled, and thinly sliced
   (see page 124)

1 tablespoon chopped fresh
   cilantro

Put the chicken in a large resealable plastic bag. Combine all the marinade ingredients in a small bowl and add to the bag with the chicken. Mix well and refrigerate overnight.

(continued on next page)

⸎ Sofrito ⸎

A flavoring base for many savory Latin American dishes, sofrito is a sautéed mixture of finely chopped onions, green pepper, garlic, and herbs. Sofrito has many variations, depending on the cuisine of origin. The Mexican version is made with tomatillos. In Puerto Rico, cilantro or *recao*, a more pungent, spicier herb, is used, and in Spain cooks sauté the aromatics with annatto seed and rendered pork fat. Sofrito is used to add flavor and depth to soups, sauces, and meat dishes.

Arroz con Pollo

(continued)

For the sofrito: Combine all the ingredients in a food processor and process until smooth. Set aside.

Preheat an oven to 375°F. Thirty minutes before cooking, remove the chicken from the refrigerator. Drain the chicken pieces and pat dry. Heat a Dutch oven or large, heavy sauté pan over medium-high heat. Add 2 tablespoons of oil and brown the chicken for 7 to 10 minutes on each side, until golden brown. Using tongs, transfer to a plate and add the onion and red bell pepper to the pan. Sauté until just tender, about 5 minutes. Stir in the sofrito and cook for 2 minutes. Add the tomato sauce, water, and salt and simmer 2 minutes more. Increase the heat to medium-high and stir in the rice and olives and bring to a boil. Return the chicken to the pan and push the chicken pieces into the rice mixture. Place the roasted red pepper strips on top, cover with aluminum foil and a tight lid, and bake for 45 minutes. Remove the lid and foil and continue to bake for 15 minutes, until the rice is tender. Garnish with cilantro and serve.

Serves 4 to 6 as a main course

Stracotto (Italian Pot Roast)

Piatti Ristorante & Bar, Mill Valley

A classic example of a perfect slow-cooked main course is Piatti's stracotto, a comforting braised dish with accents of rosemary and cloves. Piatti's serves it with braised Lacinato kale (page 160). You will need to start this dish 1 day before serving.

◦ Piatti Ristorante & Bar ◦

Focused on the bounty of local purveyors and perched in Mill Valley on the edge of Richardson Bay, Piatti is perfectly situated for diners to watch the sun setting behind Marin County's iconic Mount Tamalpais. The restaurant's menu of Italian dishes made with fresh ingredients is enhanced with a flair of northern California sophistication. Any night of the week, the bar is abuzz with regulars gathered to toast the day, while the surrounding booths and tables are filled with families, groups, and couples who celebrate well into the night.

1 (3-pound) boneless beef chuck roast, tied

1 tablespoon kosher salt

2 tablespoons olive oil

1 large yellow onion, coarsely chopped

1 carrot, peeled and coarsely chopped

2 stalks celery, coarsely chopped

5 cloves garlic, halved

2 cups canned, peeled whole tomatoes, broken up, with juice

1 tablespoon tomato paste

2 rosemary sprigs

2 cloves

2 bay leaves

4 cups beef stock

¼ teaspoon salt

⅛ teaspoon freshly ground pepper

The day before serving, salt the roast evenly with the kosher salt. Cover and refrigerate overnight.

The next day, preheat an oven to 275°F. Heat a large Dutch oven over medium-high heat. Add the olive oil and brown the beef on all sides. Transfer the roast to a plate. Pour off excess oil and sauté the onion, carrot, and celery until lightly browned. Add the garlic and sauté for another minute. Stir in the tomatoes and juice and tomato paste and cook 10 minutes more. Tie the rosemary, cloves, and bay leaves in a 4-inch square of cheese cloth. Add the herbs and stock to the sauce and season with the salt and pepper. Increase the heat to high and bring to a boil, then decrease the heat to a simmer. Return the roast to the pan and cover with a tight lid. Braise in the oven for 3 to 4 hours, or until very tender, turning the roast several times.

Remove from the oven and transfer the roast to a plate; cover and keep warm. Skim the fat off the top of the braising liquid and remove the herbs and discard. Bring the liquid to a brisk simmer over medium heat and cook to reduce by half. Taste and adjust the seasoning. To serve, cut the meat into ½-inch slices, transfer to warmed plates, and spoon the warm sauce over the roast.

Serves 4 to 6 as a main course

Cacao Nib Almond Sticks

Rustic Bakery, Larkspur

*These thin, crisp almond butter cookies are sold by the dozen at
the Rustic Bakery. The bakery uses Straus's organic butter and Scharffen Berger cacao nibs.
The sophisticated finger cookies pair well with gelato or an espresso.*

1⅓ cups all-purpose flour
1 cup sugar
½ cup blanched almonds
¼ teaspoon kosher salt
6 tablespoons cold unsalted butter
2 tablespoons water
1 teaspoon vanilla extract
⅛ teaspoon almond extract
2 ounces cacao nibs

Combine the flour, sugar, almonds, and salt in a food processor. Pulse for 4 to 5 seconds, until the mixture becomes a fine meal. Add the butter to the mixture and pulse again for 3 seconds, until the mixture is crumbly.

In a small bowl, combine the water and the vanilla and almond extracts. Add to the food processor and pulse until the dough becomes crumbly and just comes together. Add the cocoa nibs to the dough and pulse 2 to 3 quick times until just incorporated. Be careful not to overmix. Turn the dough out onto a lightly floured work surface and form into a ball. Divide the dough in half, form each half into a disk, and place each disk between 2 large sheets of parchment paper. Roll and shape each piece into a 6-by-9-inch rectangle about ¼ inch thick. Refrigerate the dough for at least 2 hours or up to 24 hours.

Preheat an oven to 325°F. Line 2 baking sheets with parchment paper. Using a sharp knife, slice the dough crosswise into ½-inch-wide strips and lay the strips 1 inch apart on the baking sheets. Bake for 8 to 9 minutes, or until a light golden brown. Let cool on the pans for 10 minutes and transfer to a wire rack to cool completely.

Makes 30 to 40 cookies

❧ Rustic Bakery ❧

When Carole LeValley emerges from her kitchen at the Rustic Bakery in Larkspur holding a platter of just-from-the-oven *pain au chocolat* or *croissants au beurre,* it's not unusual to hear waiting customers moan in anticipation. The bakery is equally well known for its flat breads—olive oil and sel gris, kalamata olive, and pepper polenta—which are baked by hand with organic ingredients.

Marin Organic Dairy Products

Milk is Marin's largest agricultural product, with at least a half-dozen organic dairies in the county—a number that is growing. Some dairies, like the well-known Straus Family Creamery of Marshall, make their own organic milk products, ranging from butter to yogurt to ice cream. Others, like the Robert Giacomini Dairy in Point Reyes Station, sell to large northern California commercial milk producers such as Clover Stornetta. Artisan cheesemakers like Cowgirl Creamery and Point Reyes Farmstead Cheese Company rely on organic milk for their products. Organic milk comes from cows that are raised in organic pastures or on organic feed and are not given any antibiotics or hormones.

Double-Chocolate Bread Pudding

Buckeye Roadhouse, Mill Valley

This dessert is a chocolate-lover's dream. The Scharffen Berger semisweet-chocolate sauce and a dollop of softly whipped cream gild the lily.

1 cup whole milk
1 cup heavy cream
4 ounces milk chocolate, chopped
5 large egg yolks
¾ cup sugar
¼ cup dark rum
¼ teaspoon vanilla extract
⅛ teaspoon salt
6 ounces semisweet chocolate
6 cups firmly packed ½-inch-diced challah or white bread (remove crusts from bread before dicing)

Chocolate Sauce

6 ounces semisweet chocolate, chopped
4 tablespoons unsalted butter
¼ cup light corn syrup
1 tablespoon brandy
¼ cup heavy cream

¼ cup hazelnuts, toasted, skinned, and chopped (see page 186) for garnish
Lightly whipped heavy cream for serving

Combine the milk, cream, and milk chocolate in a medium saucepan. Stir over medium-low heat until the chocolate is completely melted. Remove from the heat. Combine the egg yolks and sugar in a large bowl and whisk for about 5 minutes, or until pale yellow and a slowly dissolving ribbon forms on the surface when the whisk is lifted. Gradually whisk the chocolate mixture into the egg yolks. Stir in the rum, vanilla, and salt. Set the custard aside to cool.

Melt the semisweet chocolate in a large stainless-steel bowl set over a saucepan of barely simmering water. Remove from the heat and evenly fold in the bread. Pour the custard over the bread and let soak for 30 minutes.

Preheat an oven to 350°F. Butter 6 (6-ounce) ramekins or a 9-by-13-inch gratin dish. Pour the mixture into the dish(es), cover with aluminum foil, and bake for 40 to 45 minutes, or until set. Uncover and bake for another 5 minutes.

While the bread pudding bakes, make the chocolate sauce: Combine the semisweet chocolate, butter, corn

(continued on next page)

Double-Chocolate Bread Pudding

(continued)

syrup, and brandy in a double boiler over barely simmering water. Stir until melted and smooth. Remove from the heat and gradually whisk in the cream. Keep the chocolate sauce in a double warmer off the heat to keep warm.

Serve the bread pudding hot, topped with a spoonful of warm chocolate sauce, a sprinkling of toasted hazelnuts, and a dollop of whipped cream.

Serves 6

Basic Recipes

Toasting and Peeling Hazelnuts

To toast and skin hazelnuts, preheat an oven to 350°F. Place the hazelnuts on a baking sheet and toast in the oven until light golden brown, 7 to 10 minutes. Transfer the nuts to a large colander and use a tea towel to vigorously rub most the skins off the hazelnuts. The skins will fall through the holes of the colander.

Peeling, Seeding, and Chopping Tomatoes

To peel, seed, and chop tomatoes: Bring a pot of water to a boil and core the tomatoes. Carefully place the tomatoes in the water and blanch for 1 minute. Drain and let the tomatoes cool. Peel the skins from the tomatoes and slice them across the equator of the fruit. Use your fingers to remove the seeds and chop coarsely.

Segmenting Citrus

To segment citrus, use a knife to remove the skin and white pith from the fruit. Carefully slice between the membrane of each segment and remove the slices. Remove any seeds.

The following growers and producers are members of Marin Organic, a non-profit organization whose mission is to support local organic agriculture in Marin County. Proceeds of *Organic Marin: Recipes from Land to Table,* support Marin Organic's school lunch program, which helps serve 12,000 lunches a week with food grown in Marin.

Farms and Producers

Allstar Organics
P.O. Box 19
Woodacre, CA 94973
415.488.9464
www.allstarorganics.com

Big Oak Farms
5227 Red Hill Rd
Petaluma, CA 94952
707.778.6811

Blackberry Farm
77 Olema/Bolinas Rd
Bolinas, CA 94924
415.868.0683

Carbon Farm
P.O. Box 825
Nicasio, CA 94946
415.662.9820

Chileno Valley Ranch
5105 Chileno Valley Rd
Petaluma, CA 94952
707.765.3936
www.chilenobeef.com

Clark Summit Farm
P.O. Box 105
Tomales, CA 94971
707.876.3516

**Commonweal Gardens/
Regenerative Design Institute**
480 Mesa Rd
Bolinas, CA 94924
415.868.9681
www.regenerativedesign.org

Conlan Ranches California
P.O. Box 412
Valley Ford, CA 94972
707.876.1992 and 707.876.3567
www.conlanranchescalifornia.com

County Line Harvest
P.O. Box 2742
Petaluma, CA 94953
707.769.1802

Cowgirl Creamery
P.O. Box 619
Petaluma, CA 94952-2659
415.663.9335
www.cowgirlcreamery.com

Cow Track Ranch
5730 Nicasio Valley Rd
Nicasio, CA 94946
415.662.2321
www.cowtrack.net

Creekside Gardens
P.O. Box 328
Bolinas, CA 94924
415.868.1247

Drakes Bay Family Farms
17171 Sir Francis Drake Blvd
Inverness, CA 94937
415.669.1149
www.drakesbayoyster.com

Draper Farms
11 Sacramento Ave
San Anselmo, CA 94960
415.457.3431
www.onthefarm.com

Fairfax Fresh
53 Ridge Rd
Fairfax, CA 94930
415.453.5634
www.fairfaxfresh.com

Fairfax Scoop
63 Broadway
Fairfax, CA 94930
415.453.3130

Fresh Run Farm
P.O. Box 237
Bolinas, CA 94924
415.868.2313

Gospel Flat Farm
140 Olema/Bolinas Rd
Bolinas, CA 94924
415.868.0921

Green Gulch Farm
1601 Shoreline Hwy
Sausalito, CA 94965
415.354.0420
www.sfzc.org

International Harvesters
P.O. Box 841/365 Aspen Rd
Bolinas, CA 94924
www.internaturalharvesters.com

La Tercera
P.O. Box 507
Bolinas, CA 94924
415.868.0831

Little Organic Farm
1855 Tomales Rd
Petaluma, CA 94952
707.773.1338
littlefarm@sbcglobal.net

Marin Roots Farm
P.O. Box 74
Petaluma, CA 94952
415.309.2474
www.marinroots.com

McEvoy Ranch
P.O. Box 341
Petaluma, CA 94953
707.769.4101
www.mcevoyranch.com

Mostly Natives Nursery
P.O. Box 258
Tomales, CA 94971
707.878.2009
www.mostlynatives.com

Mt. Barnabe Farm
P.O. Box 468
Lagunitas, CA 94938
415.488.4746

Paradise Valley Produce
P.O. Box 382
Bolinas, CA 94924
415.868.0205

RedHill Farms
5225 B RedHill Rd
Petaluma, CA 94952
707.477.8751

Robert Giacomini Dairy
P.O. Box 1082
Point Reyes Station, CA 94956
415.663.8880
www.pointreyescheese.com

Sartori Farms
P.O. Box 32
Tomales, CA 94971
707.878.2428
www.sartorifarms.com

Slide Ranch
2025 Shoreline Hwy
Muir Beach, CA 94965
415.381.6155
www.slideranch.org

Star Route Farms
95 Olema/Bolinas Rd
Bolinas, CA 94924
415.868.1658
www.starroutefarms.com

Stewart Ranch
P.O. Box 130
Olema, CA 94950
415.663.1362

Straus Family Creamery
P.O. Box 768
Marshall, CA 94940
415.663.5464
www.strausmilk.com

Stubbs Vineyard LLC
1000 Marshall Petaluma Rd
Petaluma, CA 94952
707.486.3152
www.stubbsvineyard.com

Three Twins Ice Cream
641 Del Ganado Rd
San Rafael, CA 94903
415.492.TWIN

Wild Blue Farm
P.O. Box 83
Tomales, CA 94971
707.878.2831

Worsley Farms
P.O. Box 319
Inverness, CA 94937
415.663.1207

Bay Area Organic Food, Market, and Farm Organizations

California Federation of Certified Farmers' Markets
P.O. Box 1813
Davis, CA 95617
530.753.9999
www.cafarmersmarkets.com

Center for Urban Education About Sustainable Agriculture
One Ferry Building, Ste 50
San Francisco, CA 94111
415.291.3276
www.cuesa.org

Golden Gate Farmers' Market Association
149 Ignacio Valley Circle
Novato, CA 94949
415.382.7846

Grown in Marin
Cooperative Extension Marin County
1682 Novato Blvd, Ste 150-B
Novato, CA 94947
415.499.4204
www.growninmarin.org

Marin Agricultural Land Trust
P.O. Box 809
Point Reyes Station, CA 94956
415.663.1158
www.malt.org

Marin Farmers' Market Association
76 San Pablo Ave, Ste 200
San Rafael, CA 94903
415.472.6100
www.marincountyfarmersmarkets.org

Marin Organic
P.O. Box 962
Point Reyes Station, CA 94956
415.663.9667
www.marinorganic.org

Restaurant Contributors

AVA Restaurant
636 San Anselmo Ave
San Anselmo, CA 94960
415.453.3407
www.avamarin.com

Buckeye Roadhouse
15 Shoreline Hwy
Mill Valley, CA 94941
415.331.2600
www.buckeyeroadhouse.com

Bungalow 44
44 E. Blithedale Ave
Mill Valley, CA 94941
415.381.2500
www.bungalow44.com

Drake's Beach Café
1 Drakes Beach Rd
Inverness, CA 94937
415.669.1297
www.drakesbeachcafe.com

Farmhouse Inn and Restaurant
7871 River Rd
Forestville, CA 95436
707.887.3300
www.farmhouseinn.com

Fish
350 Harbor Dr
Sausalito, CA 94965
415.331.3474
www.331fish.com

Fork Restaurant
198 Sir Francis Drake Blvd
San Anselmo, CA 94979
415.453.9898
www.marinfork.com

Greens Restaurant
Building A, Fort Mason Center
San Francisco, CA 94102
415.771.6222
www.greensrestaurant.com

Harmony Restaurant
800 Redwood Hwy
Mill Valley, CA 94941
415.381.5300
www.harmonyrestaurantgroup.com

Incanto Italian Restaurant & Wine Bar
1550 Church St
(between 28th St & Duncan St)
San Francisco, CA 94131
415.641.4500
www.incanto.biz

Insalata's
120 Sir Francis Drake Blvd
San Anselmo, CA 94960
415.457.7700
www.insalatas.com

Kitchen
868 Grant Ave
Novato, CA 94945
415.892.6100
www.kitchen868.com

Lark Creek Inn
234 Magnolia Ave
Larkspur, CA 94939
415.924.7766
www.larkcreek.com

Lettüs Café Organic
3352 Steiner St
San Francisco, CA 94123
415.931.2777
www.lettusorganic.com

Marché aux Fleurs
23 Ross Commons
Ross, CA 94957
415.925.9200
www.marcheauxfleursrestaurant.com

MarketBar
One Ferry Building
The Embarcadero at Market St
San Francisco, CA 94111
415.434.1100
www.marketbar.com

Olema Inn & Restaurant
10000 Sir Francis Drake Blvd
Olema, CA 94950
415.663.9559
www.theolemainn.com

Piatti Ristorante & Bar
625 Redwood Hwy
Mill Valley, CA 94941
415.380.2525
www.piatti.com

Picco
320 Magnolia Ave
Larkspur, CA 94939
415.924.0300
www.restaurantpicco.com

Poggio
777 Bridgeway
Sausalito, CA 94965
415.332.7771
www.poggiotrattoria.com

Rustic Bakery
1139 Magnolia Ave
Larkspur, CA 94939
415.925.1556
www.rusticbakery.com

Scott Howard
500 Jackson St
San Francisco, CA 94133
415.956.7040
www.scotthowardsf.com

Small Shed Flatbreads
17 Madrona St
Mill Valley, CA 94941
415.383.4200
www.smallshed.com

Sol Food
732 4th St & 901 Lincoln Ave
San Rafael, CA 94901
415.451.4765
www.solfoodrestaurant.com

Table Café
1167 Magnolia Ave
Larkspur, CA 94939
415.461.6787

Index

Acknowledgments

Organic Marin: Recipes from Land to Table would not have been possible without the considerable contributions of many people.

First and foremost, we thank the farmers, ranchers, and restaurateurs who opened their fields, barns, and kitchens to us. They were as generous with their time, advice, and expertise as they are attentive to the food they produce.

Especially helpful in the writing of the book were Warren Weber of Star Route Farms, Dennis Dierks of Paradise Valley Produce, Marin Organic Executive Director Helge Hellberg, and Marin Agricultural Commissioner Stacy Carlsen.

There would be no book without the inspiration, passion, and push of Lisa Shanower, publisher of *Marin Magazine*. She not only championed the big idea, but also rode herd on the details when needed.

We relied as well on the research and organizational skills of several other *Marin* staffers, including Somer Flaherty, Alex French, Genevieve Luckel, Alex Reno, Mimi Towle, and Nancy Williams.

Jennifer Barry not only designed the book, but also provided invaluable insight into the selection of its recipes and the styling of its food photographs—not to mention a steady hand in the kitchen when called upon.

Food stylist Jackie Slade prepared the recipes for photography in her San Rafael studio, doing the hard work of taking them from raw ingredients to finished presentations. A host of friends, family, and *Marin Magazine* staff members were kind enough to loan us their beautiful plates, platters, and tableware to serve as props in the photos.

Finally, thanks also to Andrews McMeel publisher Kirsty Melville, who adopted the project as her own; editor Lane Butler, who saved us from our occasional excesses; and licensing consultant Mary Sullivan, who helped us make the publishing connection that started it all.

—Tim Porter and Farina Wong Kingsley